COOKING ROCKS!

RACHAEL RAY
30-MINUTE MEALS
FOR KIDS

By Rachael Ray

Illustrated By Chris Kalb

Lake Isle Press, Inc.   New York

Published by Lake Isle Press, Inc.
16 West 32nd St., Suite 10-B
New York, NY 10001
lakeisle@earthlink.net

Distributed to the trade by:
National Book Network (NBN), Inc.
4501 Forbes Boulevard, Suite 200
Lanham, MD 20706
1(800)462-6420
http://www.nbnbooks.com

Library of Congress Control Number: 2004111102
ISBN: 1-891105-15-9

Small portions of this book previously appeared in *The Open House Cookbook* by
Rachael Ray, 1999, Lake Isle Press, Inc.

Photography: Jean-Claude Dhien, courtesy of the Food Network
Book and cover design: Chris Kalb

A word of thanks to the children whose drawings of Rachael appear in this book.
Just a few pictures were selected from the many she receives, but she (and we)
think you all do wonderful work.

This book is available at special sales discounts for bulk purchases
as premiums or special editions, including personalized covers.
For more information, contact the publisher: (212)273-0796 or by e-mail.

10 9 8 7 6 5 4 3 2 1

~DEDICATION~

To cool kids everywhere who love to eat and COOK!

Good luck with your picky-eater parents.
These recipes should teach them a thing or two
about your good taste.

Also, thanks to my family
for not letting me become a picky eater
and for teaching me that
COOKING ROCKS!

Table of Contents

Heads Up to Grown-ups!

People often ask me where and when I learned to cook. The truth is, I never did. No one "taught" me how to cook. No one person ever showed me how to hold a knife or how to tell when chicken was done. No one explained to me which flavors were good together and which were not. How then did I learn? The answer has to do with my family.

The kitchen was the center of my childhood home. As kids, my brother and sister and I were spoiled in an unusual way. We were treated as respected members of the group. All the adults in our home listened when we spoke, giving us the same attention they gave other adults. In turn, when they spoke, we listened.

This is not to say that we were treated as adults. We were treated as children, with rules to follow, and were taught right from wrong. But, when given a direction to follow, we were spoken to in a way that assumed we were capable. "Rachael, clean the potatoes and add them to the pot, please" is a very different statement from, "Rachael, can you clean the potatoes?" We were made to feel confident in our own abilities. We felt a responsibility to figure out how to do things for ourselves. I work with this in mind to this day. I look at a task at hand and say to myself, "I can figure this out." Then I get busy and figure it out.

Cooking can give kids a wonderful sense of accomplishment. They can see the results of their labors and creativity immediately — tangible, great-tasting food that others can share and enjoy. Kids develop a real sense of pride when given a pat on the back for something they did all by themselves, despite their small size and age.

How young is too young? You are never too young to be in the kitchen. My mother stirred her pots with me hanging off her hip. She would play music and hum and dance around the kitchen to Melody of Love (Montovani, of course) while she moved mountains, platters, and pots full of food! My sister Maria had my nephew Nicky in the kitchen next to her, on a baby stepping stool, at just 2 years of age. She gave him a plastic knife to pretend chop right alongside her. Today, at 4, he uses a small real knife to cut up tiny bits of soft vegetables and cheeses. And Sabia, my best friend Vicky's daughter, has been using a chef's knife since she was 6! Of course you need to keep a watchful eye of the stove and small fingers, always reminding children to keep their fingers tucked in when they use any blade. But if you let them explore and contribute in the kitchen from an early age, you'll be amazed at the ideas kids can come up with!

When it comes to ideas for your child's next party, cooking is cool! Gathering a group of kids together to cook is a triple treat for everyone. Activities are all taken care of — cooking is the name of this party game. Parents are happy because picky eaters aren't so picky when it's their food on the table. And at party's end, everyone has learned something not only about food, but something about themselves, too. So, round up the troops and skip lunch, the kids are cooking tonight!

Grown-ups, LISTEN UP!

Keep your cool!

Never grab a kid's arm or speak harshly to a kid cook unless he or she is in real danger of burn or injury. Let them make mistakes. You can always scoop out too much of something, add a little more of something else, or start from scratch if necessary. All of these options are better solutions than making kids feel as self-conscious as so many adults are about cooking. Food should be fun. Cooking is a celebration of all the good things we have to be thankful for in life, including little kids.

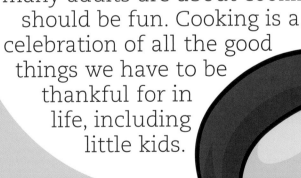

WHY COOKING ROCKS!

I was really psyched to write this book because so many of you guys watch my show, 30 Minute Meals! I love all the awesome ideas I get from all of you, so please keep them coming!

I have been cooking since I was really little and it has made my life really tasty, not to mention that it turned out to be a really cool job, too! Why not try? I wanted this book to be different from other kids' cookbooks. Often the food and recipes are made to seem like a joke, all about making animals or clowns out of pizza or sandwiches. I've tried to write really good recipes that people of all ages will enjoy making. You can keep on cooking all this stuff even when you are technically not a kid anymore. In fact, there is not one recipe in here that I would not prepare or eat, even today.

Cooking when you are a kid is cool. It can help you find your independence. It's fun to be young, but it kinda stinks that you have no car or money of your own. But, when you cook, you can make something really good for yourself or the ones you love, and it won't cost anything more than the groceries in the kitchen. Cooking can also help you figure out your own true likes and dislikes, and you can learn to experiment and have fun with all the foods and spices from around the world. So don't be shy. Give everything a try!

Knowing how to cook is fun when you are a little kid because it feels like playing, and then you get to eat the toys.
When you get older, cooking becomes really useful in many ways. When you know how to cook, you always have the perfect gift for any occasion! Moms love a Mother's Day breakfast in bed and any Dad would be thrilled with a big Father's Day dinner on the grill or maybe a picnic! When your brothers, sisters, or grandparents have a birthday or graduation or anniversary, make them a spaghetti supper or maybe a nice juicy steak to celebrate! They'll love it.

If you start cooking when you're really young, by the time you're ready for college, you'll be a chef in your own right!
You'll be able to cook for dates (the way to anyone's heart is still through his or her stomach) or cook for your dorm mates on weekends and sell your suppers for $5 bucks a plate! Just a thought....

At 35 and counting, I still love to cook and I cook every night, when I am home. Cooking relaxes me and lets me express myself. It's like drawing a really cool picture or writing a song, but I get to eat my creation when I'm done.

Cooking can also become your life's scrapbook.

I use some recipes to remind me of special people and places I love and miss. One day, when you're living far from home, you'll find that nothing in the world will make you happier or feel better than the memory of your favorite recipe that your mom or dad used to make for you when you were little.

Food can help you remember the best times of your life. Learn how to cook and you'll be thankful and forever full!

Heads Up, Kids!

Here's some stuff to know before you go into the book or the kitchen:

What's a GH?

Grown-up Helpers, or GHs, can help out with steps in recipes that are a little beyond your skills or strengths, mostly for those of you under 11. The smaller we are, the more we can use some big, strong helpers. It's kinda fun to push around your GHs, but remember to say thank you, too!

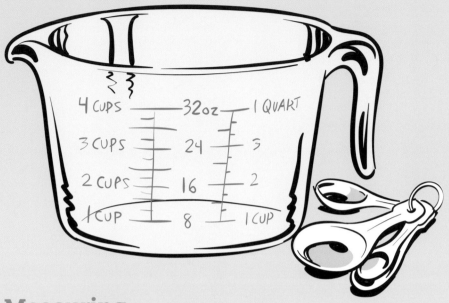

Measuring

Measuring can teach us lots about math and fractions and stuff, but my mom never really measured anything, so I don't measure either, except when I try to bake (not my strong point). Anyway, I always "eyeball" my measurements, which means I estimate (take a good guess at) the amount by using my eyes and fingers. As a beginner, it's a good idea to use measuring tools until your eyes get to know and understand what a teaspoon or tablespoon of something actually looks like. Then, as you cook more often, you can learn to estimate, too. I have come up with some guidelines to some measurements: a tablespoon of oil is about 1 turn around the pan in a slow, steady stream, a tablespoon of a dried spice is a palmful, etc. You'll come up with your own system, too, once you figure out how you like your food to taste. Pretty soon you'll be eyeballing it all!

Knives and Cutting

Know your size! Only use a knife that feels comfortable in your hand. I know 7-year-olds who use huge chef's knives and 37-year-olds who chop everything with small paring knives! It's all about what works best for you.

Remember:

- Always keep a firm hold on what you are chopping, and keep your eyes on your hands—don't look away until you put the knife down.
- Keep your fingers curled under when you hold what you are chopping so you don't nick them as you work. Cut down and away from your body, tilting the blade slightly away from your body as you chop. Don't "saw."
- Give round things such as tomatoes or carrots "feet" by making a small thin slice on one side of the vegetable so that it sits flat or upright and won't roll when you chop it.
- Always keep your knives sharp.
- Also, try kitchen shears! Snipping can be much easier and just as effective as chopping.

Clean Like You Mean It!

Clean pots and dishes as you cook so you don't have a ton of clean up afterwards.

Use plastic boards to chop raw meats because plastic can be thoroughly cleaned. When handling raw meats it is very important to wash your hands, your cutting board, and your utensils with antibacterial soap before doing anything else.

Keep a nail brush at the sink to get any gunk out from under your fingernails, too.

KITCHEN

Scissors

I love using scissors in the kitchen and if you aren't quite up to the chopping stage yet, scissors can be really helpful! Use them to snip fresh herbs and to cut veggies such as green onions and bell peppers. You can also trim pastry dough and open plastic packaging with them. Buy some scissors just for kitchen use; even really little kids can use child safety scissors with rounded tips.

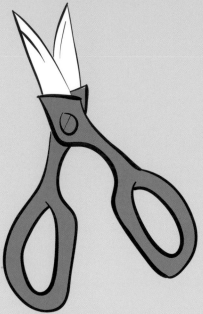

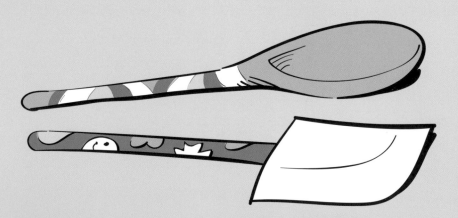

Wooden Spoons or Rubber Spatulas

Each young cook should have his or her own wooden spoon or rubber spatula (heat-safe) to stir with. Decorate the handles with stickers or paints to let everyone else know whose spoon is whose!

BASICS

A Garbage Bowl

Put a big bowl on the counter next to where you are working. Rather than running back and forth to the garbage can with your scraps and wrappers, pile them into the garbage bowl as you work. Then when you are done cooking, you can empty the bowl at once.

A BIG Cutting Board

A big wooden cutting board is a good thing to have. First, you have more room to work, so you can make separate piles of ingredients as you chop, and save yourself from dirtying a bunch of little bowls. Also, big boards are so heavy that they won't move around on you. And, if possible, place this board next to the stovetop. Then, you can chop and drop ingredients right into the pot as you work.

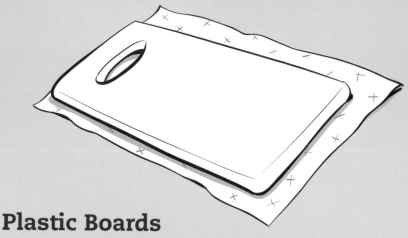

Plastic Boards

As I've said before, use plastic boards for handling raw meat of any kind as they're easier to fully clean. Remember, too, to place a wet paper towel underneath a plastic board to keep it from sliding around. Plastic boards are not as heavy as wooden ones, and they can move around on you, making it tricky to chop.

Rolling Pins and Small, Heavy Pans

Rolling pins are cool because you can use them for a lot of tasks other than baking. For example, place stale bread or toast in a bag and roll over it to make bread crumbs or you can do the same with nuts, cookies, crackers, or cereals to make ingredients for use in recipes. And I don't have to tell you that you can place flour on the counter and use the rolling pin to roll out pizza dough.

Small heavy skillets are handy for other things beyond frying, too. You can use them to pound chicken cutlets to make them thinner or to **squish garlic** out and away from its skin or to weigh down panini (sandwiches), pressing them while they toast in a pan.

SECTION 1

Recipes for ages →

4+

Also, feel free to make these same recipes if you are way older, too. I am 35 and I still make them all.

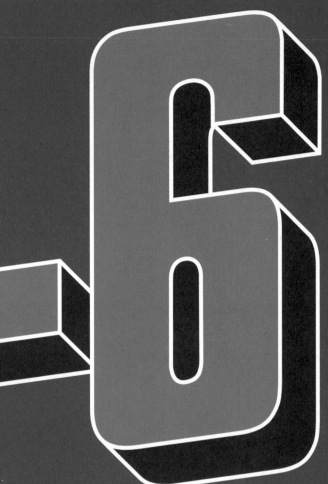

with a GH
(Grown-up Helper)

Hot Dog Pizzas and Minute Pickles

■ Makes 4 servings; 2 bagel pizzas each and 4 minute-pickle spears each

PIZZAS

4	large plain, egg, or sesame bagels, split in half by GH (Grown-up Helper)
1 bottle	ketchup with squirt top
1 sack	preshredded cheddar cheese (available on dairy aisle)
2	hot dogs, sliced by GH
	Scallions, snipped with kitchen scissors, for garnish (optional)
	Sweet or dill pickle relish, for garnish (optional)

PICKLES

1 teaspoon	sugar
1 tablespoon	grill seasoning blend, such as Montreal Steak Seasoning by McCormick
2	Kirby cucumbers (small pickling cucumbers) or 1 English seedless cucumber

Make the pizzas: Have your GH place a rack in the center of the oven and preheat the broiler. Place the bagels on a cookie sheet and put them in the oven to toast. When the bagels are toasted have the GH pull them out. Let the toasted bagels cool, 5 minutes. Have the GH switch the oven setting to 400°F.

Squirt ketchup all around each bagel; it's your hot dog pizza sauce. Top the bagels with lots of cheddar cheese. Arrange the sliced hot dogs like pepperoni on a pizza, putting the slices all over the top of each bagel. Have the GH put the pizzas back in the oven and cook them until the cheese is bubbly and the hot dog slices are hot, 5 to 6 minutes.

While the pizzas are baking, make the pickles: Put sugar and grill seasoning in a small bowl and mix together. Have the GH cut the cucumbers into spears about 4 inches long. Use your hands to gently sprinkle your special spice blend over the spears.

Have the GH take the pizzas out of the oven and slide them onto a cutting board. Dot pizzas with snipped scallions and relish, or serve plain. Cut pizzas into wedges and serve with minute-pickle spears.

Dawg-Gone Good Menu

Italian Alphabet Soup + Cheesy Soup Dippers

■ **Makes 4 servings**

1 wedge	**Parmigiano Reggiano cheese with the rind on**
2 cloves	**garlic, in the skins**
2 tablespoons	**extra-virgin olive oil (evoo)** (2 turns of the pot)
1 small	**onion, chopped by GH** (Grown-up Helper)
1 cup	**marinara or tomato sauce**
5 cups	**chicken stock** (1 quart-size box and one 8-ounce box)
1 cup	**alphabet pasta**
2 jumbo	**English muffins, cut open by GH**
2 tablespoons	**butter** (tablespoons are marked on the wrapper)
	Garlic powder
	Dried Italian seasoning blend
1 cup	**frozen peas and carrots or 1 cup frozen mixed vegetables** (lima beans, cut green beans, peas, carrots, and corn)
	Salt and freshly ground black pepper, to taste

Have your GH get you a box grater and set it on a cutting board. Shred up lots of Parmigiano Reggiano cheese for topping your bread dippers and for topping your soup. You'll need 1 to 1 & 1/2 cups; that'll be a pile about as high as your hand if you stand it up next to the cheese. Ask the GH to trim off the rind of the cheese for you and save it; you will put it into the soup later, which will make the whole soup taste as good as the cheese. The cheese rind is your SECRET ingredient, so tell the GH not to tell anyone else.

SOUPER SOUP MENU

Ask the GH to put a medium soup pot over medium heat. Place the garlic cloves onto a cutting board and get a small, heavy frying pan from your GH. Use both arms and hit the garlic, one clove at a time—WHACK! Pull the skins away from the garlic and throw them away.

Count for your GH as they add 2 turns of the pan of evoo in a slow stream to the soup pot. Throw in the garlic and onions and stir with a long wooden spoon. Let the onions and garlic cook 2 or 3 minutes. Add the tomato sauce and stir. **Have the GH pour in the chicken stock slowly, so it does not spatter or splash out.** Give it a stir, put a lid on the pot, and turn up the heat to high to get it to boil. When the soup boils, let the GH take the lid off the pot with a pot holder, then let them stir in the alphabet pasta and the cheese rind you've been saving (the SECRET ingredient). Reduce the heat to medium-low and simmer (let the soup bubble and cook). Cook until the pasta letters are just tender, 6 to 7 minutes.

While the soup cooks, toast up the English muffins in your toaster oven. While they toast, melt the butter by putting it in the microwave for 15 seconds on high. Have the GH take the dish out in case it's hot. Brush toasted muffins with butter, then sprinkle with lots of the cheese you grated and some garlic powder and Italian seasoning. Have the GH put the muffins on the toasting tray and into the toaster oven to melt the cheese on top. Have the GH cut the garlic-cheese muffins into 2-inch strips, 4 strips per muffin half. Use these cheesy strips to dip into your soup.

Have the GH cool a noodle for you to test and see if it's done. Maybe they can pick out the same letter that you start your name with. I always test an R for Rachael. When you say the pasta is about done, add the vegetables and a little pepper. Cool a few spoonfuls of soup and check the taste to see if it needs extra pepper or a little salt. Take the cheese rind out of the soup and serve.

Serve bowls of your Italian alphabet soup with a few dippers to dunk and extra grated cheese to sprinkle on top.

Orange

Green apple

chocolate milk

strawberry

spaghetti & meatballs

Fresh herbs

Brownie

Holding Hands

Rachael

Abby

Cake

banana

Artwork
by **Abby**

Crunchy Oven-Baked CHICKEN TOES!

■ **Makes 4 servings**

1 cup	**corn flakes cereal, any brand**
1 cup	**plain bread crumbs**
2 tablespoons	**brown sugar**
1 teaspoon	**salt**
1/2 teaspoon	**freshly ground black pepper**
1/2 teaspoon	**allspice** (the SECRET ingredient)
3 tablespoons	**vegetable oil**
1/3 cup	**all-purpose flour**
2	**eggs, beaten**
1 + 1/2 pounds	**chicken breast tenders** (2 packages), **cut into 2-inch pieces by GH** (Grown-up Helper)
1/4 cup	**honey mustard, such as Gulden's brand**
1/4 cup	**barbecue sauce, any brand**

Have your GH turn the oven on to 375°F.

Make the breading: Pour the corn flakes into a pie pan or other large, shallow dish. Crush the cereal up with your hands. Mix in bread crumbs, brown sugar, salt, pepper, and allspice (your SECRET ingredient; do not tell anybody what your secret ingredient is—ever!).

Drizzle the vegetable oil evenly over the breading. **Have the GH pour the oil out slowly.** A vegetable oil bottle has a big opening, so 3 tablespoons will pour out pretty quickly, probably by the time you can count to 5, so watch the GH closely and count really

Me, with my friend Beauchamp.
Gotta watch your GH very carefully!

loudly! Toss and turn it to mix the oil all through the bread crumbs and crushed-up corn flakes.

Pour the flour into another shallow dish, and the beaten eggs into a third. Turn the chicken in flour, then eggs, and then in the special crunchy breading. Arrange the chicken toes on a nonstick baking sheet. **You and your GH should go and wash your hands now.** Place the chicken toes in the oven and cook until crisp and brown all over, about 15 minutes. Work on the other stuff in this menu—the veggies and the apples and dip—while the toes are cooking in the oven.

When the toes come out of the oven, it's time to stir up the sauce for dipping them. Mix together honey mustard and barbecue sauce in a small bowl. Dip your hot chicken toes into your honey mustard barbecue sauce.

Creamy SALSA Dip and Veggies

■ **Makes 4 servings**

1 cup	**mild salsa, any brand**
1/2 cup	**sour cream**
12	**carrot sticks, store-bought or cut by your GH** (Grown-up Helper)
12	**celery sticks, store-bought or cut by your GH**
12	**cherry or grape tomatoes**
12	**sugar snap peas**

Make the dip: Stir together salsa and sour cream. Scrape the dip into a small bowl. Put the small bowl in the middle of a big plate. Arrange the veggies all around the dip and serve.

The Big Dipper Menu

3 Courses, No Silverware!

Creamy Salsa Dip and Veggies

Crunchy OvenBaked Chicken Toes

Fuji Apples and Peanutbuttery Caramel Dip

FUJI APPLES and Peanutbuttery Caramel Dip

■ **Makes 4 servings**

24	**wrapped caramel candies** (1/2 of a 14-ounce bag), such as Kraft brand
2	**Fuji apples**
2 tablespoons	**freshly squeezed lemon juice** (from about 1/4 lemon)
1 cup + 1 tablespoon	**water**
2 tablespoons	**creamy peanut butter**
Pinch of	**cinnamon** (this is your SECRET ingredient)

Unwrap candies and place in a bowl. While you are working on that, have your GH cut the apples into quarters then cut out the seeds. The GH should then slice apples into 8 pieces per apple. Count for them; you'll need 16 slices altogether. Squirt the lemon juice into a bowl and add 1 cup water to it. Add the sliced apples to the water and turn them around in it, then drain them in a strainer or colander. Lemon juice is sour, but it's only a tiny bit on lots of apple slices. The apples will still taste sweet and really good. The lemon juice keeps the apple slices from turning brown.

Add 1 tablespoon water and the peanut butter to the caramel candies. Place candies into the microwave oven and cook them on high for 2 minutes. Stir up the dip with a rubber spatula. If the candy is not melted all the way, put it back in the microwave on high for another 20 seconds. Add a pinch of cinnamon to the sauce and stir. DO NOT TELL ANYONE ABOUT THE CINNAMON! Tell your GH not to tell, too. This is your secret ingredient.

To serve, place the drained, sliced apples next to the peanutbuttery caramel dip and dip away! To reheat the dip, place it back in the microwave for 30 seconds.

PASTA and TREES

■ **Makes 4 servings**

1 pound	**broccoli tops**
	Salt and freshly ground black pepper, to taste
1 pound	**pasta: penne rigate, corkscrew cavatappi, elbows, or medium shells**
1 tablespoon	**extra-virgin olive oil (evoo)**
2 tablespoons	**butter, cut up** (tablespoons are marked on the wrapper)
1 cup	**grated parmesan, Parmigiano Reggiano, or Romano cheese**

EASY CHEESY DINNER!

Have your GH (Grown-up Helper) put a big pot of water on to boil for the pasta.

Separate the broccoli into small trees by pulling them apart. Ask your GH to trim off the woody stems of your trees so you can break them up right. Put the broccoli florets (trees) into a pot and have the GH add water enough to just cover the tops. The GH should bring the water to a boil and add 4 pinches salt to the water; you can count for them. Cook the broccoli 5 minutes and have the GH drain it.

When the pasta water boils, have the GH put 4 pinches salt into the pot and add pasta. Cook to al dente (that's Italian for "done but still with a bite to it"), according to the package directions.

Put the evoo and butter in a big bowl. Have the GH add the hot drained pasta and broccoli to the bowl. Add the cheese to the bowl and stir it all up until the butter melts and the cheese mixes in. Add a little salt and pepper and taste the pasta and trees to see how the seasoning is.

PASTA, CHEESE, and TREES
My Mama's Way

EASY CHEESY ITALIAN DINNER!

■ **Makes 4 servings**

1 pound	**broccoli tops**
	Salt and freshly ground black pepper, to taste
1 pound	**pasta: penne rigate, corkscrew cavatappi, elbows, or medium shells**
1 tablespoon	**extra-virgin olive oil (evoo)**
2 tablespoons	**butter, cut up** (tablespoons are marked on the wrapper)
3 cloves	**garlic, chopped by GH**
1 cup	**ricotta cheese**
1/2 cup	**grated parmesan, Parmigiano Reggiano, or Romano cheese**

Have the GH put a big pot of water on to boil for the pasta.

Separate the broccoli into small trees by pulling them apart. Ask your GH to trim off the woody stems of your trees so you can break them up right. Put the broccoli florets (trees) into a pot and have the GH add water enough to just cover the tops. The GH should bring the water to a boil and add 4 pinches salt to the water; you can count for them. The broccoli should cook about 5 minutes once the water comes to a boil. Then have your GH drain it.

When the pasta water boils, have them put 4 pinches of salt into the pot and add pasta. Cook to al dente (that's Italian for "done but still with a bite to it"), according to package directions.

Pour oil and butter into a deep frying pan and let the GH heat it up over low heat. When the butter melts, they can add the garlic and cook it 5 minutes. Have the GH add the broccoli to the garlic.

Have the GH drain the pasta and add to broccoli. Add the ricotta and grated cheese, and have the GH stir it all up in the big frying pan. Add a little salt and pepper and taste the pasta and trees to see how the seasoning is.

My mom adds garlic and ricotta cheese to this dish. This is the way I had my pasta and trees when I was little—and I still do today.

Fruit Benedicts and Egg Scrambles

■ **Makes 4 servings**

FRUIT BENEDICTS

4	**English muffins, split by your GH**
	Creamy peanut butter
1 cup	**crushed pineapple**
1	**banana, sliced by your GH**

SCRAMBLES

8	**eggs**
4 stems	**chives** (long, thin, green herbs that taste like yummy sweet onions)
4 pinches	**salt**
4 grinds	**black pepper**
4 slices	**Canadian-style bacon** (round thin slices of ham)
2 tablespoons	**butter** (tablespoons are marked on the wrapper)
1 + 1/4 cups	**shredded cheddar cheese** (half a 10-ounce sack; preshredded is available on the dairy aisle)

Make the fruit benedicts: Have the GH heat the broiler. Put the English muffin pieces on a cookie sheet and have the GH toast them in the middle of the oven on both sides. While they are warm but not too hot to touch, spread each half with peanut butter. Put spoonfuls of pineapple on each muffin on top of the peanut butter and then put sliced bananas on top of the pineapple. Put the fruit benedicts on a platter to serve.

Breakfast for Dinner, Menu 1

Make the scrambles: Have the GH heat a nonstick skillet over medium heat. Crack the eggs into a bowl (can you help crack them?). Use your kitchen scissors to snip the chives into the bowl with the eggs. Add salt and pepper and beat up the eggs with a whisk. If the yolks won't break, poke them with a fork. When the eggs are mixed, use your scissors again to chop up the ham slices into little pieces, and keep them on the cutting board. The GH should add butter to the hot skillet and when it melts, add the ham you cut up. Cook ham 2 minutes. The GH can add your eggs and chives now and stir until they are scrambled, cooked, and the ham is hot all through. Add cheese and stir into eggs to melt it.

Serve eggs with fruit benedicts and eat.

Use some kid-safe scissors that you have just for the kitchen to make these super scrambles. The fruit benedicts make a great snack, too, or even a dessert!

Birds in a Nest with Blankets

■ **Makes 4 servings**

4 slices	**bread, white or wheat**
2 tablespoons	**butter** (tablespoons are marked on wrapper)
4	**eggs**
	Salt and freshly ground pepper, to taste
4 deli slices	**Swiss or cheddar cheese**

Use a round cookie cutter to cut out a hole in the center of 4 slices of bread. Remove the holes.

Have a GH (Grown-up Helper) heat a large nonstick skillet over medium heat. Put butter in the pan and let it melt. Have your GH arrange the bread in the pan for you. Next, have the GH crack 1 egg and drop it in the hole of 1 slice of bread. Repeat with the remaining eggs and bread. Keep count for the GH until all 4 holes are filled. The eggs are the birds and they nest in the bread! Season the eggs with salt and pepper and cover the pan with foil to cook eggs on top, too.

When eggs are cooked, top the birds in their nests with cheese blankets and replace the foil loosely on top of the pan to melt the cheese.

BREAKFAST OR BREAKFAST-FOR-DINNER MENU 2

birds in a nest with blankets

yogurt and sliced fruit

Yogurt and Sliced Fruit

■ **Makes 4 servings**

4 cups	**strawberry-banana yogurt**
1 cup	**granola**
1	**banana, sliced**
4	**strawberries, hulled** (cut off the green parts)**, sliced**

Place 1 cup yogurt in each of 4 bowls and top with granola, sliced bananas, and strawberries.

Yogurt served this way is like having an ice cream sundae, but it's good for you. Plus, you can eat it at breakfast, lunch, or dinnertime!

Spinach & 3-Cheese Panini, Italian Flag Panini (Red, White, Green) with Tomato, Cheese, and Basil Pesto, & Pizza Panini

■ **Makes 4 servings; 3 half-sandwiches per person**

2 cloves	**garlic, in skins**
1/2 cup	**extra-virgin olive oil (evoo), eyeball or estimate the amount**
1 box	**frozen spinach, defrosted in the microwave** (10 ounces)
1/2 cup	**ricotta cheese** (half a small container)
1/2 cup	**grated parmesan or Parmigiano Reggiano cheese**
4 slices	**provolone from the deli**
1 large round loaf	**crusty Italian bread, sliced at bread counter**
	Salt and freshly ground black pepper, to taste
1/2 cup	**pesto sauce** (a super-yummy green herb and cheese sauce that's available in the dairy aisle in tubs)
2 small	**plum tomatoes, seeded and diced by your GH** (Grown-up Helper)
1 pound	**fresh mozzarella, chopped by GH into small cubes**
1/2 cup	**pizza sauce, any kind**
6 slices	**salami**
12 slices	**pepperoni** (like for pizza)

You will build 2 panini of each kind, for 6 panini total. When they are all made, the GH can cook them up and help you serve them. Each person can have 1 half-sandwich of each kind.

Start by putting garlic cloves on a cutting board. Hit each one with

Panini

Panini is what Italian kids call sandwiches. Sometimes the sandwiches are hot like grilled cheeses. They are really good and make a fast dinner when no one wants to cook. You and your friends and family can make a whole meal out of these sandwiches and call it a Panini Party! You can eat panini for lunch or dinner, so have fun and happy eating! There are a lot of panini to make, so let friends or even sisters and brothers help.

a small, heavy skillet and give the garlic a good WHACK! Throw the skins into the garbage bowl. Add the garlic to the evoo in a microwave-safe bowl and put it in the microwave. Cook it 25 seconds on high and let it sit there until you need it. Because you heated the oil and garlic together, all the oil will taste like yummy garlic, so your sandwiches will taste like they are made on garlic bread—cool!

For the spinach and cheese panini, put the defrosted spinach into a kitchen towel and squeeze out all the juice to make the spinach dry. Mix the ricotta and parmesan together in a small bowl. Line up the spinach, the cheese mix, and the sliced provolone. Get a pastry brush and the sliced bread. Get the garlic oil from the microwave. Brush one side of four slices of the bread with garlic oil and put the painted side down on the cutting board. Place half the drained spinach on each of 2 slices of bread, pulling it all apart and spreading it out. Season it with salt and pepper. Top with cheese mix in equal amounts and 2 slices provolone. Put the other 2 pieces of bread on top to make a sandwich with the oiled sides facing up.

For Italian flag panini, start out the same way, painting 4 slices of bread. Spread pesto sauce on two slices of bread and top with tomatoes and half the diced mozzarella. Season the fillings with salt and pepper. Top the sandwiches with the other 2 slices, keeping the oiled side up.

You've got the hang of this now! The pizza panini sandwiches are the same. Start by painting your bread with the oil. Then spread the pizza sauce on 2 slices. Put 3 slices salami and 6 slices pepperoni on top of the sauce, then add the rest of the mozzarella to the two sandwiches and put the tops in place.

Hand off the rest of the work to the GH.

Cooking instructions for GH's:
If you have a panini press, just press your young chef's panini in batches until toasted and melted. If you do not have a press, cook panini on a nonstick pan over medium heat using a brick, covered in foil, or a cast-iron skillet to weight and press them. They cook 2 to 3 minutes on each side. Cut each sandwich in half and pile on a huge platter to serve.

Lunch Box Turkey "Sushi"

1/2 cup	**Minute Rice**
1	**spinach flour tortilla, any brand**
2–3 tablespoons	**ranch or Russian dressing**
3–4 slices	**turkey breast from deli**
A handful of	**pea shoots or bean sprouts**
2	**red bell pepper strips, 1/4 inch wide**
2 slices	**deli-cut cheddar or provolone cheese, cut into 1/2-inch strips**
	Salt and freshly ground black pepper, to taste

Have your GH (Grown-up Helper) prepare Minute Rice according to package directions, maybe while they make their morning coffee.

Heat a flour tortilla for 15 to 20 seconds on high in the microwave oven. Spread out tortilla on a work surface. Coat the tortilla evenly with dressing. Cover with slices of turkey. Pile some rice onto one side of the turkey. Arrange the pea shoots, pepper strips, and cheese strips in a line on top of the rice. Season it up with salt and pepper. Wrap and roll the sandwich up around the rice, veggies, and turkey, making the ingredients resemble a sushi roll with the cheese and veggies at the center of the rice. Cut the sandwich wrap into 2-inch-long pieces. Arrange in Tupperware or on aluminum foil and pack up for your school lunch.

I ♥

RACHEL
RAE

Best cook

hands
down!

— ♥ your youngest fan

JADE

5 yrs. old
Lakeland, MN

49

SECTION 2

Recipes for ages 7+

Chicken Catch-a-tory Ravioli Stew

■ **Makes 4 servings**

3 cloves	**garlic, skins on**
2 tablespoons	**extra-virgin olive oil (evoo)** (twice around the pan in a slow stream)
2 stems	**fresh rosemary**
2 stems	**fresh thyme**
1 cup	**presliced fresh mushrooms** (about 1/3 pound) **have GH** (Grown-up Helper) **slice for you**
	Salt and freshly ground black pepper, to taste
1 can	**stewed tomatoes with peppers, onions, and celery** (15 ounces)
2	**roasted red peppers from a jar, drained**
1 cup	**tomato sauce**
1 package	**chopped frozen spinach, defrosted in microwave and drained** (10 ounces)
6 cups	**chicken broth**
3/4 – 1 pound	**chicken breast tenders** (1 package)
1 pound	**fresh ravioli, any flavor**
1 cup	**grated parmesan, Parmigiano Reggiano or Romano cheese, to pass at table**
	Crusty Italian bread or rolls, to pass at table

Nice Italian Menu
for the Family
— — — —
Chicken Catch-a-tory
Ravioli Stew

A Nice Italian Girl's
Salad (...but boys
can make it, too!)

Have your GH heat a medium soup pot over medium-high heat.

Place 3 cloves of garlic on a cutting board and WHACK each clove with a small heavy frying pan. Pick out the skins and chuck them in your garbage bowl. **Have the GH add evoo, 2 turns of the pan, to the soup pot.** Throw in the smashed garlic and 2 stems each of the

This recipe was especially designed for Sabia Rose to make for Bill and Vicki, 'cause she's Daddy's AND Mommy's Little Girl — and a really good cook, too!

rosemary and fresh thyme herbs. The leaves will fall off the stems and give a delicious flavor to your special stew. Add the mushrooms, too, and help stir as the mushrooms cook 3 to 5 minutes. Season the 'shrooms up with salt and pepper as they're cooking.

Next, you or your GH can open the can of stewed tomatoes and add them to the pot. Use a sharp, small knife to chop the roasted red bell peppers. Keep your fingers on the hand holding the peppers curled under so you don't chop off a whole finger! You just want to cut up those peppers into pieces as big as your mouth; that's what they call bite-size. Add the chopped-up roasted red peppers and add 1 cup tomato sauce to the soup pot.

Put defrosted chopped spinach in a kitchen towel. Gather towel up and twist it to get the water out of the spinach. Squeeze the spinach over your garbage bowl until it stops dripping. Separate spinach with your fingers and add it to the soup. Pour in chicken broth and stir the stew really slowly or it will slosh out of your pot! Have the GH cover the soup and raise the heat to high.

Have the GH cut up the chicken for you on a separate plastic cutting board from the one you cut up the vegetables on. Cut the chicken tenders into 1-inch pieces, and add them to the stew. Tell the GH to go wash up right away with lots of soap and hot water—including the board—so that the raw chicken doesn't get on anything else in the kitchen or any other food. If you touched the raw chicken, you should wash up, too.

When the stew comes up to a boil again, add the ravioli and leave the lid off. Cook stew until the ravioli is almost done, about 5 minutes. Turn off the heat and let the stew cool down a little bit. **Have your GH serve up the stew and pass cheese and bread at the table to go with it.**

A Nice Italian Girl's Salad

■ **Makes 4 servings**

1 sack	**chopped romaine lettuce** (10 ounces) (available in the produce aisle)
1/2 cup	**black pitted olives** (available in the fancy olive bins near the deli)
1	**roasted red pepper from a jar, drained and sliced**
12 grape	**tomatoes**
24 slices	**pepperoni**

ITALIAN BLENDER DRESSING

3 tablespoons	**red wine vinegar** (about 3 splashes)
2 tablespoons	**green salad olives with red pimientos and juice**
6	**fresh basil leaves, torn up**
2 to 3 tablespoons	**fresh flat-leaf parsley leaves** (a handful)
3 big spoonfuls	**grated parmesan, Parmigiano Reggiano, or Romano cheese**
	Freshly ground black pepper, to taste
1/2 cup	**extra-virgin olive oil (evoo), eyeball it**

Wash your hands. Pour lettuce into a big salad bowl. Break up the olives a little with your fingers. Scatter the olives and the sliced red peppers around the salad. Add in the grape tomatoes and pepperoni slices, too.

Make the dressing: Pour the vinegar into a blender. Add the olives, basil, parsley, cheese, pepper, and evoo. **Have the GH (Grown-up Helper) place the lid on the blender and blend the dressing until everything is all chopped up and mixed up together.** Pour dressing over the salad and toss it up good.

Worms and Eyeballs

■ **Makes 4 servings**

1 pound	**bucatini** (hollow spaghetti that looks just like worms)
1 small	**red bell pepper**
1 + 1/2 pounds	**ground chicken breast** (1 package)
2 cloves	**garlic, chopped**
2	**tablespoons chopped ginger**
2	**scallions, finely chopped**
2 tablespoons	**hoisin sauce** (Chinese-style barbecue sauce, available on Asian foods aisle)
	Salt and freshly ground black pepper, to taste
3 tablespoons	**vegetable oil**
1 cup	**preshredded carrots** (available in the produce department)
1 cup	**bean sprouts** (a couple handfuls)
1 cup	**snow pea pods, cut into pieces with kitchen scissors or knife**
1/2 cup	**tamari** (dark soy sauce), **eyeball it**

Have your GH preheat the oven to 400°F. Put a large pot of water on to boil for the pasta. Cut off about a quarter of the bell pepper, **and have your GH chop it finely.** Slice the rest of the pepper yourself.

Combine the chicken, garlic, ginger, scallions, finely chopped red bell pepper, hoisin sauce, salt, and pepper in a bowl. Roll the mixture into meatballs the size of chicken eyeballs and place balls on a nonstick cookie sheet, coated lightly with 1 tablespoon of vegetable oil. Roast the chicken eyeballs 10 to 12 minutes.

When the pasta water comes to a boil, add the pasta and cook according to package directions, just until al dente, that is, with a bite left to it—just like Dracula would like, right?

When the pasta is almost cooked through and the meatballs are about 5 minutes from coming out of the oven, start stir-frying the veggies. **If you are not used to cooking at the stove, have the GH do the frying of the veggies, you can hand them the veggies as they need them.** Heat a large nonstick skillet over high heat and add the remaining 2 tablespoons vegetable oil (2 turns of the pan). Add the sliced red bell pepper, the carrots, sprouts, and pea pods. Stir-fry veggies 1 minute. **Have the GH drain the noodles and add the worms to the vegetables.** You pour in the tamari while the GH tosses the worms and veggies to combine and evenly coat.

Transfer noodles to a serving platter. Remove the eyeballs from the oven and roll them on top of the worms, then serve.

If a fussy eater in your family wants to know "What's in this?" just say "Worms and eyeballs! Hungry?" This tasty meal makes any day seem as spooky as Halloween night! Boo!

CANDY "SUSHI"

■ **Makes 4 servings**

1 tablespoon	**butter, cut into pieces** (tablespoons are marked on the wrapper)
12	**marshmallows**
2 cups	**puffed rice cereal, such as Kellogg's Rice Krispies**
6	**fruit roll-ups** (pressed dried fruit rounds, 6 inches wide) **any brand, any flavor**
6	**strips licorice, such as Twizzler's brand, cut in half**

Melt butter in a medium saucepan over low heat and add marshmallows. Stir marshmallows until completely melted. Remove mixture from heat and add cereal. Stir to coat cereal evenly in melted marshmallows.

Roll out the fruit roll-ups. Place a few spoonfuls of the coated cereal onto each fruit roll-up and gather toward the back edge of the roll-up. Press 2 cut licorice twists onto cereal mix. Wrap and roll the candy and fruit roll-up so that the finished product resembles a sushi roll, shimmying the licorice into the center of the Rice Krispies.

Place a sharp knife into a bowl of very warm water. Cut candy sushi with warm knife and arrange pieces on a plate to serve. The candy sushi looks like a big platter of California sushi rolls! This is one trick that makes a tasty treat!

Tricks & Treats Menu

Worms and Eyeballs
Candy "Sushi"

Rice Bowl Menus!

If you are interested in learning more about the flavors used in cooking all around the world, these rice bowls are a fun way to explore. Each dish can be a one-pot meal: veggies, tofu, chicken, or shrimp with rice—and only one dirty pot to clean! However, if you do the cooking, you should totally get out of doing the dishes, no matter what.

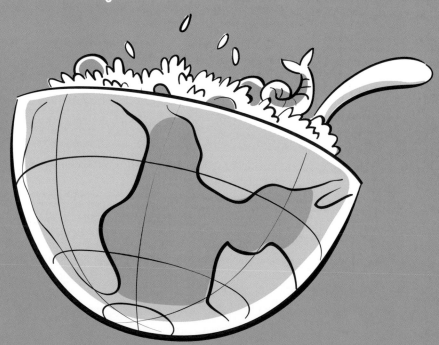

Mexican Rice Bowl

■ **Makes 4 servings**

1 tablespoon	**extra-virgin olive oil (evoo)** (one turn of the pan)
2 tablespoons	**butter** (tablespoons are marked on the wrapper)
3/4 pound	**chicken tenders, cut into bite-size pieces**
	Salt and freshly ground pepper, to taste
2 cups	**white rice**
1 quart	**chicken stock**
1 tablespoon	**Sazon seasoning blend by Goya** (available in Mexican and Spanish foods section)
1/2 cup	**tomato salsa or taco sauce**
1/4 cup	**drained chopped olives and pimentos** (salad olives)
2 tablespoons	**chopped fresh flat-leaf parsley** (a handful)
	Blue or red corn tortilla chips and salsa, for serving (optional)

Heat a medium pot over medium heat; add evoo and butter. When butter has melted into oil, add cut-up chicken tenders. (**Your GH, or Grown-up Helper, can chop for you if you are not comfortable enough with your knife yet.** Remember: All fingers should be tucked under; keep knife blade tilted away from your body; use a knife that matches your size and skill level. Wash your hands, knife, and board after handling the raw chicken pieces.) Season the chicken with salt and pepper. Sauté the chicken, stirring, until lightly browned. Add the rice and cook another minute or two. Then add chicken stock to the pot and Sazon seasoning. Put a lid on the pot and raise the heat to high to bring the stock to a quick boil, 2 or 3 minutes. When the liquid boils, reduce heat to simmer and put the lid back on. Cook until rice is tender but still a little chewy in the center, 13 to 15 minutes.

Take off the lid and stir in salsa or taco sauce, olives and pimentos, and parsley. Turn off heat and let stand 5 minutes. Serve hot Mexican rice in bowls placed on dinner plates and garnish plates with chips and leftover salsa or taco sauce for dipping.

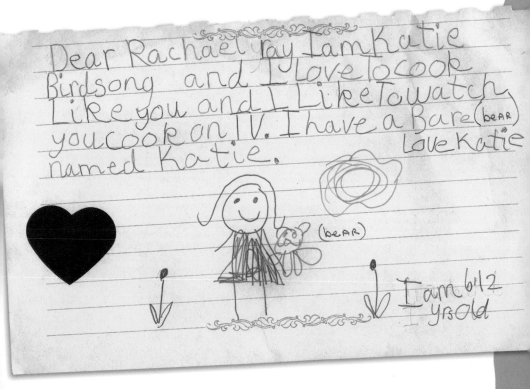

Dear Rachael Ray I am Katie Birdsong and I Love to cook Like you and I Like To watch you cook on TV. I have a Bare (beAR) named Katie.

Love Katie

(beAR)

I am 6 1/2 yrs Old

Artwork by Katie

Middle Eastern Rice Bowl

■ **Makes 4 servings**

1 tablespoon	**extra-virgin olive oil (evoo)** (one turn of the pan)
2 tablespoons	**butter** (tablespoons are marked on the wrapper)
3/4 pound	**chicken tenders, cut into bite-size pieces**
	Salt and freshly ground pepper, to taste
2 boxes	**Near East brand rice pilaf mix** (6 ounces each) (rice and toasted pasta called orzo)
3 cups	**chicken stock**
1/2 teaspoon	**ground cinnamon**
2 tablespoons	**chopped fresh flat-leaf parsley** (a handful)
1/2 cup	**slivered almonds**
2 cups	**store-bought hummus** (my favorite is 40 Spice Hummus by Tribe of Two Sheiks, but any variety will do), **for serving** (optional)
1 bag	**pita chips** (available on snack aisle), **for serving** (optional)
	Trimmed scallions, for serving (optional)
1	**red bell pepper, cut into strips, for serving** (optional)
	Cucumber sticks or disks, for serving (optional)

Heat a medium pot over medium heat; add evoo and butter. When butter has melted into oil, add cut-up chicken tenders. (**Your GH, or Grown-up Helper, can chop for you if you are not comfortable enough with your knife yet.** Remember: All fingers should be tucked under; keep knife blade tilted away from your body; use a knife that matches your size and skill level. Wash your hands, knife, and board after handling the raw chicken pieces.) Season the chicken with salt and pepper. Sauté the chicken, stirring, until lightly browned. Add the rice pilaf and cook another minute or 2. Add chicken stock. You do not need to use the seasoning packets included in the rice mix; you'll get your flavor from cooking the rice in chicken stock. Put a lid on the pot and raise the heat to high to bring the stock to a quick boil, then reduce to a simmer. Cook until rice is tender, about 15 minutes.

Take off the lid and stir in cinnamon, parsley, and almonds. Serve rice in bowls with veggies, pita chips, and hummus on the side.

My sister Maria makes this dish in memory of our Grandma Betar's cooking. As children, we loved Grandma Betar and her wonderful Middle Eastern cooking. Now that we are grown, my sister is really good at keeping Grandma Betar with us all through the preparation of such recipes. Today, Maria's own kids, Nick and Jess, love Middle Eastern dishes like this one.

Thai Rice Bowl

■ **Makes 4 servings**

2 cloves	**garlic**
2 tablespoons	**vegetable oil** (2 turns of the pan in a slow stream)
1/2 pound	**chicken cutlets, cut into bite-size pieces**
1/2	**red bell pepper, chopped or cut with kitchen scissors into small pieces**
2 teaspoons	**Thai fish sauce** (2 squirts) (available on Asian foods aisle)
	Freshly ground pepper, to taste
2 cups	**water**
1 can	**chicken stock**
2 cups	**jasmine rice** (available on international foods aisle)
2 cups	**300-count baby shrimp** (that means 300 shrimp are in one pound)
3	**scallions**
20 leaves	**fresh basil**

CUCUMBER SALAD (optional)

1/2	**cucumber, sliced**
1/2 cup	**carrots, shredded**
1 tablespoon	**sugar**
1 teaspoon	**salt**
2 tablespoons	**white vinegar**
1 tablespoon	**oil**

Whack garlic cloves with a small heavy skillet. Pick out the skins and throw them away. Chop up the garlic, carefully **(your GH, or Grown-up Helper, can do this for you if you're not comfortable with your knife skills)**. Try placing the tip of a knife on the cutting board and hold it in place with one hand while you lift the handle

up and down over the garlic with your other hand. Keep the hand pressing the knife tip on the board nice and flat and firm, making sure your fingertips do not come near the cutting edge.

Preheat a medium pot over medium-high heat; add vegetable oil and chopped chicken. Wash your hands. (**Your GH can chop chicken for you.** When chopping, remember: All fingers should be tucked under; keep knife blade tilted away from your body; use a knife that matches your size and skill level. Wash your hands, knife, and board after handling raw chicken.) Add red bell pepper, fish sauce, and black pepper. Add water and chicken stock. Put a lid on the pot and raise the heat to high to bring the liquid to a boil. When the liquid boils, add the rice. When the liquid returns to a boil, reduce heat to simmer and cover the pot. Cook 15 minutes.

Add baby shrimp and stir. Cook another 5 minutes. Remove the pot from the heat and, using scissors, chop scallions and thin slices of basil over the pot. Stir once again and serve as is or with cucumber salad on the side. (Combine all ingredients in a bowl.)

Chinese Rice Bowl

■ **Makes 4 servings**

3 cups	**water**
1 + 1/2 cups	**short-grain white rice**
	Store-bought vegetable spring rolls (available in frozen foods section), **for serving** (optional)
1/4 cup	**tamari** (dark, sweet soy sauce), **plus more for dipping spring rolls, eyeball it**
2 teaspoons to 1 tablespoon	**toasted sesame oil** (tastes and smells kind of like peanut butter), **eyeball it**
2	**scallions, chopped with kitchen scissors into small pieces**
1 pound	**medium or firm tofu, cut into cubes**
1 tablespoon	**sesame seeds** (I think of these like candy sprinkles for Asian food!)

Bring water to a boil over high heat. Add rice and return to a boil. Place lid on pot and reduce heat to simmer; cook until tender, about 18 minutes.

If you would like to serve some vegetable spring rolls with this rice bowl, prepare them while rice is cooking, according to package directions, in a toaster oven or microwave.

In a bowl, combine tamari, sesame oil, and scallions. Add tofu and toss to coat in sauce.

Using a large ice cream scoop, place scoops of plain rice in bowls and top with tofu and sauce, then sprinkle the bowls with sesame seeds to garnish. Serve alone or with spring rolls on the side with extra tamari for dipping.

Sloppy Turkey Joes

■ **Makes 4 servings**

1 + 1/3 pounds	**ground turkey or ground turkey breast** (1 package)
2 tablespoons	**extra-virgin olive oil (evoo)** (2 turns of the pan)
1/2	**red onion**
1/2	**red bell pepper**
1 tablespoon	**grill seasoning blend** (a palmful), **such as Montreal Seasoning by McCormick or Mrs. Dash grill seasoning for poultry**
2 tablespoons	**brown sugar**
1 tablespoon	**Worcestershire sauce**
1 cup	**tomato sauce** (8 ounces)
4	**crusty sandwich rolls, split**
12	**celery sticks** (available in produce department, or GH can chop)
12	**carrot sticks** (available in produce department, or GH can chop)

Using a pair of kitchen scissors, cut open the package of ground turkey and hand it off to your GH (Grown-up Helper).

Have your GH place a big skillet over medium-high heat for you. Add the evoo. **Have the GH add the ground turkey to the pan, in case it spatters.** Break the turkey up with a big wooden spoon as it starts to cook. If anyone touches the raw turkey, they should go wash their hands.

If you are a really good chopper, using a small, sharp knife chop up some red onion. Remember when you are chopping to keep the fingers that are not holding the knife all tucked in and curled under. **Have a GH help you.** You need half a red onion chopped up

I wrote this one for my guy, Tyler! He's too cool! His mom, Melanie, works really hard on our show, 30 Minute Meals. Now Tyler can make a 30 Minute Meal for her!

small. Pull the seeds and white membrane and the top out of a half red bell pepper and chop that up small too. Add the veggies to the cooking meat and stir it all together.

Next, mix in a small bowl: grill seasoning blend, brown sugar, Worcestershire sauce and the tomato sauce. This will make your special sauce. When all the ingredients are combined, pour the sauce evenly over the meat and stir everything together really well. Turn the heat down to simmer and cook the sloppy mixture for 10 minutes. Blow on a spoonful until cool and taste it to see if you need to adjust the seasoning.

Have the GH help you serve. Place bun bottoms on plates. Use a big ice cream scoop to get a pile of sloppy meat onto each bun. Put bun tops in place and serve with vegetable sticks on the side and cheese fries (see recipe on next page).

Cheese Fries

■ **Makes 4 to 6 servings**

1 sack	**frozen french fries, any brand or shape, prepared to package directions.**
2 tablespoons	**butter** (tablespoons are marked on the wrapper)
2 tablespoons	**all-purpose flour**
1 + 1/2 cups	**whole milk**
2 + 1/2 cups	**shredded yellow cheddar cheese** (one 10-ounce sack, preshredded, available on the dairy aisle)
1/4 cup ketchup	(about 3 squirts)

Read the package directions to see what temperature to set the oven at, and **have your GH (Grown-up Helper) preheat the oven.**

Have your GH put the fries on a cookie sheet and put that in the oven. Read the package directions to see how long to cook the fries, and set the oven timer. While fries are baking, have a GH place a saucepan on the stove and heat it over medium heat. Add butter and melt it. Add the flour and stir. Cook butter and flour together for 1 minute or so. This is called roux (sounds like Roo, Tigger and Pooh Bear's friend), and it helps to thicken up sauces.

Weeknight Bite Menu

Sloppy Turkey Joes

Cheese Fries

Use a whisk to stir as you pour the milk into the pot. Keep stirring until the milk gets thicker. Use a wooden spoon or heat-safe spatula to stir in the cheese. When all of the cheese melts, take the sauce off the heat and stir in 3 squirts ketchup. This is your SECRET ingredient. When everyone asks what you put in your cheese sauce that makes it taste so good, just say milk and cheese, you can NEVER tell what secret ingredients you add! Tell your GH to keep the secret, too, or they can never help you again!

Pour the cheese sauce over the fries or serve the sauce on the side if you like dipping better.

This is a wicked-easy recipe that's wicked-good!

Quesadilla Pizzas!

■ **Makes 4 servings**

8 large	**flour tortillas** (10-inch)
2 + 1/2 cups	**shredded cheddar cheese** (one 10-ounce sack, preshredded is available on dairy aisle)
1 cup	**salsa, red or green, mild or hot**
3/4 pound	**brick smoked cheddar or pepper-Jack cheese**
1/2 cup	**sliced green olives and pimentos, drained**
3	**scallions, cut up with kitchen scissors or chopped into small pieces**
8 ounces	**chorizo or linguiça sausage** (available near kielbasa in meat department), **thinly sliced or diced**

Preheat oven to 400°F. Take out 2 nonstick cookie sheets. Place 2 tortillas on each cookie sheet, one next to the other. Top each tortilla with lots of cheddar cheese. Place another tortilla on top of each cheese-covered tortilla. Put the tortillas in the oven and bake 5 minutes.

Take them back out of the oven using pot holders. Press the tortillas down a bit with a spatula to set them in place with the melted cheese. Top each cheese quesadilla with some salsa, a sprinkle of smoked cheddar or pepper-Jack cheese, olives, pimentos, scallions, and some thin slices of chorizo or linguiça. Put the pizzas into the oven and cook until edges are brown and crisp and cheese is melted on top, 5 or 6 minutes more. Take the pizzas out and transfer 1 whole pizza onto each dinner plate to serve.

3-Colored Salad

■ **Makes 4 servings**

1	**heart of romaine lettuce** (light green to white)
1 bundle	**arugula lettuce** (dark green and spicy)
1 small	**head radicchio** (purple-red and slightly bitter—in a good way!)
1 tablespoon	**balsamic vinegar, eyeball it**
1 tablespoon	**honey**
3 tablespoons	**extra-virgin olive oil (evoo)**
	Salt and freshly ground pepper, to taste

Tear or chop romaine and put it in a salad bowl. Cut up arugula with your kitchen scissors and add to the bowl. Thinly slice up the radicchio (you can have your GH, or Grown-up Helper do this for you if you're not comfortable with your knife skills) and add that to the bowl, too.

In a small bowl, whisk together the vinegar and honey; then, while you whisk, have a GH stream in the evoo for you.

When you are ready to eat, pour dressing over the salad and toss. Season salad with salt and pepper.

COOKING ROCKS! PARTY POINTER

A little music adds to any party and relaxes every cook. Mix it up! Play a little samba and swing along with kids' favorites. Kids can bring their own chart-topping tapes or disks to the gathering and take turns sharing their tastes.

Green Noodles & Ham

■ **Makes 4 servings**

1 box	**spinach fettuccine pasta** (12–14 ounces)
1/4 pound	**prosciutto** (Italian ham)
3 tablespoons	**butter** (tablespoons are marked on the wrapper), **cut into small pieces**
1 cup	**cream or half-and-half**
1 to 1 + 1/2 cups	**grated Romano or Parmigiano Reggiano cheese**
	Salt and freshly ground pepper, to taste
1 cup	**frozen green peas, thawed**

Bring a big pot of water to a boil and add a spoonful of salt to the water to season the pasta as it cooks. When it boils, add pasta to the water and cook according to package directions to al dente (done, but with a bite to it).

Fast Feast menu

3-colored salad

green noodles and ham

While the pasta cooks, cut prosciutto into thin, short, ribbonlike pieces using kitchen scissors. Separate ham ribbons, loosely pile them up, and set aside.

Preheat a large skillet over moderate heat. Place butter in pan to melt. Add 1 cup cream or half-and-half. Stirring constantly, add 1 cup cheese and cook sauce 1 minute, seasoning with pepper and a pinch of salt.

Turn off heat under sauce and **have a GH (Grown-up Helper) drain pasta for you.** Add pasta and defrosted peas to the skillet. Toss pasta until sauce coats the noodles evenly. Add prosciutto ribbons and toss to evenly distribute them. Taste the pasta and, if you think it needs it, melt in even more cheese, up to 1/2 cup. When the pasta tastes just perfect, start serving it up! Mangia! (That means "eat" in Italian.) Wow! Spinach green noodles are even yummier than white ones when you eat them with ham!

This meal is a FEAST and it's super fast: The sauce cooks in just one minute—really! And it's made with ingredients most of us have in the house: butter, half-and-half, and grated cheese.

Bite-Size Antipast-Salad

■ **Makes 4 servings**

DRESSING

1 tablespoon	**balsamic vinegar**
2 tablespoons	**extra-virgin olive oil (evoo)**
	Salt and freshly ground pepper, to taste
1/4 pound	**chunk provolone cheese, cut into pieces**
1/2 pound	**bocconcini** (bite-size fresh mozzarella pieces), **pieces cut or snipped in half** (available in fancy cheese section)
1	**whole roasted red pepper, chopped or snipped into pieces** (available in jars or at the deli counter)
1 can	**quartered artichoke hearts in water, drained**
12 slices	**pepperoni**
1/4 pound	**salami, sliced, chopped into bite-size pieces**
1/2 cup	**olives, pitted black or green** (good quality, from bulk bins)
1/2 pint	**grape tomatoes**
1	**heart of romaine lettuce, chopped or torn into bite-size pieces**
10	**leaves fresh basil, torn or snipped into slivers**

Make the dressing: Whisk vinegar and oil together in a small bowl until combined. Add salt and pepper and whisk again.

Combine cheeses, red pepper, artichoke hearts, meat, olives, tomatoes, lettuce, and basil on a shallow platter pour dressing over. Season the salad with salt and pepper.

81

MINI SHRIMP SCAMPI
and Angel Hair Pasta

■ **Makes 4 servings**

1 pound	**angel hair pasta**
4 cloves	**garlic**
2 tablespoons	**extra-virgin olive oil (evoo)** (2 turns of the pan)
3 tablespoons	**butter** (tablespoons are marked on the wrapper), **cut into small pieces**
1 pound	**300-count baby shrimp** (that means there are 300 shrimp to a pound)
	Salt and freshly ground pepper, to taste
1 cup	**chicken stock**
4 to 5 blades	**chives, snipped with scissors** (2 tablespoons)
	A handful of fresh flat-leaf parsley leaves, chopped or snipped (2 tablespoons)

Tiny Menu
with
Big Flavor

Bite-Size
Antipast-Salad
Mini Shrimp Scampi
and Angel Hair
Pasta

Put a large pot of water over high heat and bring to a boil; add salt. Cook pasta according to package directions, to al dente.

Meanwhile, smash garlic cloves with a small pan; separate out the skins and throw them away.

Heat a large skillet over medium heat. Add evoo and butter. When butter has melted into oil, add crushed garlic and cook 2

minutes. Add shrimp; add salt and pepper. Cook shrimp until heated through, 2 or 3 minutes; add stock and raise up heat to bring to a boil. **When liquid boils, remove pan from heat and have the GH (Grown-up Helper) drain pasta and add to the pan.** Toss pasta with shrimp, sauce, and the snipped or chopped herbs. Adjust seasonings and serve.

SMASHED Potatoes and Cream Cheese!

■ **Makes 6 servings**

2 + 1/2 pounds	small red potatoes or baby Yukon gold potatoes
1/2 cup	half-and-half or whole milk
8 ounces	plain cream cheese or veggie cream cheese, cut into pieces
10	chives
or 2	scallions, chopped or snipped with kitchen scissors
	Salt and freshly ground pepper, to taste

Place potatoes in a pot of water over high heat and boil until potatoes are tender, about 15 minutes. Have your GH (Grown-up Helper) drain them and return them to the hot pot to let them dry out a bit. Mash potatoes with half-and-half or milk using a potato smasher. The GH can get the mash going for you. Add the cream cheese and smash until the cheese melts into the potatoes some, then add chives or scallions and season with salt and pepper.

While the water boils and when the potatoes are cooking, you can be working on the meatloaf recipe.

Making Mac & Cheese Rachael Style :-)

RACHAEL RAY

TO RACHAEL RAY
, 2004   ALExandra

Meatloaf Muffins with Barbecue Sauce

■ **Makes 6 servings**

	Vegetable oil or extra-virgin olive oil (evoo), for pan
1 + 1/2 pounds	ground sirloin
1 small	yellow onion, cut into quarters
1 small	green bell pepper
A splash	of milk
1 large	egg, beaten
1 cup	plain bread crumbs
2 tablespoons	grill seasoning, such as Montreal Steak Seasoning by McCormick
1 cup	smoky barbecue sauce
1/2 cup	tomato salsa
1 tablespoon	Worcestershire sauce

Preheat oven to 450°F. Brush a 6-muffin tin with vegetable oil or evoo.

Put ground beef into a big bowl. Put onions into a food processor. Cut the bell pepper in half and rip out the seeds and the white stuff and throw it away. Cut the pepper into a few pieces and add to the food processor. Pulse the processor blades to finely chop the onion

meɡa-comfort food menu

smashed potatoes and cream cheese

meatloaf muffins with barbecue sauce

micro-way-cool green beans and bacon

and bell pepper. Add to the meat bowl. Whisk the milk into the beaten egg, and add to meat. Add bread crumbs and grill seasoning.

In a small bowl, mix together the barbecue sauce, salsa, and Worcestershire sauce. Pour half the sauce mixture into the bowl with the meatloaf mix. Mix the meatloaf together with your hands. Wash your hands well. Use a large ice cream scoop to put the meat into muffin tin. Top each meatloaf muffin with a spoonful of reserved sauce. Bake about 15 minutes. **Have a GH (Grown-up Helper) cut open one muffin to test if it's cooked through.** While meatloaf muffins bake, make green beans in the microwave (see next page). Serve meatloaf with smashed potatoes and cheese on the side, too.

Micro-way-cool Green Beans & Bacon!

■ **Makes 6 servings**

6 slices **microwave ready-crisp bacon**
1 bag **frozen green beans (16 ounces)**
Extra-virgin olive oil (evoo), for drizzling
Salt and freshly ground pepper, to taste

Place bacon between paper towels and microwave 60 seconds on high. Cool bacon and chop or crumble it up.

Place green beans in a bowl and drizzle with evoo; add salt and pepper. Cover the bowl loosely with plastic wrap and microwave green beans on high for 5 minutes, stir and cook 5 minutes more. Remove wrap and top green beans with crumbled bacon.

BLANKET-IN-A-PIG

■ **Makes 8 pieces**

1 can	**soft breadstick dough** (available in the dairy case)
1/2 cup	**grated parmesan, Parmigiano Reggiano, or Romano cheese, eyeball it**
2 tablespoons	**honey, eyeball it**
2 tablespoons	**deli-style mustard, such as Guldens**
8 slices	**smoked or honey ham or smoked turkey or honey roast**

Preheat oven according to the directions on the package of soft breadsticks. Open the breadstick package and separate the sticks. Pour the grated cheese onto a plate. Roll each breadstick in cheese, pressing lightly to make it stick. Place the bread-sticks on a nonstick baking sheet and continue baking according to package instructions. Remove from oven when golden (10 to 12 minutes, depending on brand) and allow the soft breadsticks to cool slightly.

Party Nite
Bites,
Menu 1

Blanket-
in-a-Pig

Cheesy
Fun-due

Mix the honey and mustard in a small bowl. Lay out 4 slices of meat on a work surface and spread each with honey-mustard. Place a bread-stick on one end of the deli slice and wrap and roll the meat up and around the bread stick. Repeat with remaining 4 breadsticks.

Cheesy FUN-due

■ **Makes 6 servings**

2 tablespoons	**all-purpose flour**
1 + 1/4 cups	**whole milk or half-and-half**
1 teaspoon	**onion powder**
1 teaspoon	**granulated garlic** (or powder)
1 pound	**Swiss cheese, grated**
1 pound	**sharp cheddar cheese, shredded** (preshredded is available on dairy aisle)
Juice of 1	**lemon** (squeeze the juice from a cut lemon upright so that the seeds remain with the lemon, not in your dip)
2 cups	**broccoli florets** (just the tops) (available in produce department)
1/2 pound	**baby carrots** (available in produce department)
1 small	**to medium zucchini, cut into disks**
1 bag	**pita chips, plain, onion, garlic, or herb flavor** (available on the snack aisle)
	Cooked shrimp, for dipping (optional)
	Cooked mini-franks, for dipping (optional)
	Cut up leftover meats, for dipping (optional)
	Cubed day-old breads, for dipping (optional)
	Cut-up rotisserie turkey breast, for dipping (optional)
	Chicken pieces, for dipping (optional)

Put the flour in a large, microwave-safe bowl. Pour in 1/4 cup of the milk (eyeball the amount) and whisk until very smooth. Add the rest of the milk to the bowl; add the onion and garlic powders and whisk again until the mixture is smooth. Microwave on high until very hot, but not boiling, 2 minutes. Remove sauce from the microwave and whisk again until smooth. Add cheeses and lemon juice, stirring until combined, then return the bowl to microwave and cook on high for 5 minutes. Remove the bowl from the microwave and stir the cheese sauce until all of the cheese is melted and the sauce is smooth again. **Ask a GH (Grown-up Helper) to help if you get pooped out.**

Transfer sauce to a fondue pot or a smaller microwave-safe bowl. Place the fondue pot or small bowl on a large platter or board and surround with veggies and pita chips and any optional dippers you like. If the sauce gets thick, return to microwave for a minute to remelt it a bit.

Mini Cheeseburger Pizzas American Style

■ **Makes 4 servings (8 mini cheeseburger pizzas)**

You'll need a 3-inch round cookie cutter with a sharp edge to make these pizzas.

1 pound	**ground beef**
2 teaspoons	**Worcestershire sauce, eyeball the amount**
2 teaspoons	**grill seasoning, such as McCormick Montreal Steak Seasoning, or salt and freshly ground pepper**
1	**shallot, chopped, or 1 scallion, cut into thin slices with your kitchen scissors**
	Extra-virgin olive oil (evoo), for drizzling
1 brick	**cheddar cheese** (you will use about 4 ounces of it)
1	**thin-crust pizza shell, such as Boboli brand**
	Ketchup
	Mustard
4 mini	**gherkin pickles, sliced**

PARTY NITE BITES MENU 2

Mini Cheeseburger Pizzas, American Style or Italian Style

Baby Tomatoes, Zucchini, and Romaine Hearts with Caesar Dressing Dip

Preheat the broiler and make sure the oven rack is in the center of the oven.

Mix together ground beef, Worcestershire, grill seasoning, and shallot or scallion. Break the meat mixture in half and from each pile make 4 large meatballs. Squish the meatballs flat to make them into mini hamburger patties. Wash your hands. Heat a large nonstick skillet or a grill pan over medium-high heat. Grill the patties in a little evoo, 2 minutes on each side **(have your GH, or Grown-up Helper check them for doneness)**. Cut 8 slices of cheddar cheese large enough to cover the mini burgers.

Use the cookie cutter to cut out eight 3-inch circles of pizza crust. Place the pizza crust circles on a cookie sheet and place the mini burgers on top. Arrange the cheese on the burgers and put them in the oven to melt cheese and warm the crust.

Top cooked mini cheeseburgers with squirts of ketchup, mustard, and sliced mini pickles.

Mini Cheeseburger Pizzas Italian Style

■ **Makes 4 servings (8 mini cheeseburger pizzas)**

You'll need a 3-inch round cookie cutter with a sharp edge to make these pizzas.

1 pound	**ground beef**
1/4 cup	**grated parmesan, Parmigiano Reggiano, or Romano cheese** (a couple of handfuls)
2 teaspoons	**grill seasoning, such as McCormick Montreal Steak Seasoning, or salt and freshly ground pepper**
1	**shallot, chopped, or 1 scallion cut into thin slices with kitchen scissors**
	Extra-virgin olive oil (evoo), for pan
4 deli slices	**provolone cheese**
1	**thin-crust pizza shell, such as Boboli brand**
1 cup	**pizza sauce or spaghetti sauce**
8 slices	**pepperoni**

Preheat the broiler and make sure the oven rack is in the center of the oven.

Mix together ground beef, grated cheese, grill seasoning, and shallot or scallion. Break the meat mixture in half and from each pile make 4 large meatballs. Squish the meatballs flat to make them into mini hamburger patties. Wash your hands. Heat a large nonstick skillet or a grill pan over medium-high heat. Grill the patties in a little evoo for 2 minutes on each side **(have your GH, or Grown-up Helper check them for doneness)**. Pile the sliced provolone up and cut across to make half-moons, then cut in half again to make wedges.

Use the cookie cutter to cut out eight 3-inch circles of pizza crust. Place the pizza crust circles on a cookie sheet and place a spoonful of pizza sauce on each, then place the mini burgers on top. Place 2 wedges provolone on each burger and one slice pepperoni on top of the cheese. Put the mini pizza cheeseburgers in the oven to melt cheese and warm the crust.

Baby Tomatoes, Zucchini, and Romaine Hearts with Caesar Dressing Dip

■ **Makes 4 to 6 servings**

12 mini	vine-ripe tomatoes or cherry tomatoes, or 24 grape tomatoes
1 medium	zucchini, cut into disks
1	heart of romaine lettuce, bottom cut off and leaves separated
1/2 cup	store-bought light Caesar dressing, such as Ken's Steak House brand
1 cup	sour cream or plain yogurt

Arrange veggies on a platter. Pour dressing into a small dip bowl and stir with sour cream or plain yogurt, then place on platter with veggies. Dip veggies and lettuce pieces into dressing as you eat them.

This makes an easy and fun alternative to tossed salad for serving with your mini cheeseburgers.

You're Great!

Dear Miss. Ray,
My name is Hattie Mae
Wilkinson. You are a great
role modle. I read your
book instead of storys,
You're great and a great
cook.

From
Hattie.

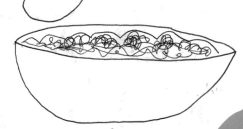

Monte Cristo and ELVIS* French Toast Sammies!

■ **Makes 4 servings**

8 slices	thin sandwich bread, such as Pepperidge Farm brand
4 slices	deli Swiss cheese
2 slices	deli turkey
2 slices	deli ham
1/4 cup	peanut butter
1 small	banana, sliced
2	eggs, beaten
2 splashes	milk
2 tablespoons	butter (tablespoons are marked on the wrapper)
	Maple syrup, for dipping

Make the Monte Cristos: On a slice of bread, stack 1 slice Swiss cheese, 1 slice turkey folded in half, 1 slice ham folded in half, another slice Swiss, and another slice bread. Make 2 Monte Cristo sandwiches.

Make the Elvis sandwiches: Spread the remaining slices of bread with peanut butter. Top 2 slices with pieces of banana and place sandwich tops in place, using the peanut butter as glue to hold the sandwiches together.

Heat a nonstick skillet over medium heat. Mix together eggs and milk. Add a tablespoon of butter to the pan and melt it. Dip all 4 sandwiches into egg mixture then cook the French toast sammies in the skillet until golden, 3 or 4 minutes on each side (flip with a spatula, **or have your GH, or Grown-up Helper, do it**). While sammies cook, warm maple syrup in the microwave on high for 30 seconds in a microwave-safe pitcher. Pour the warm syrup into small cups and serve with sammies. Cut each sammy from corner to corner and serve half an Elvis and half a Monte Cristo per person.

Variations: Try making peanut butter and jelly French toast sandwiches or peanut butter and bacon French toast sandwiches. Make them the same way you make the Elvis sammies, just change the fillings.

NOW SHOWING

BREAKFAST OR BREAKFAST-FOR-DINNER MENU 3

MONTE CRISTO & ELVIS FRENCH TOAST SAMMIES

TROPICAL YOGURT PARFAITS

Tropical Yogurt Parfaits!

■ **Makes 4 servings**

2 cups	**custard-style vanilla yogurt** (low-fat or nonfat)
1 small can	**mandarin oranges, drained**
1 cup	**crispy rice breakfast cereal, any brand**
1 small can	**crushed pineapple**

Put a couple of tablespoons of yogurt in the bottom of 4 juice glasses. Top with mandarin orange slices and a few spoonfuls each of crispy rice and crushed pineapple. Add more yogurt to fill up the glasses and top off with another layer of fruit and crispy rice. Cool! These dessert parfaits work for your breakfast or your dinner!

Ham-and-Egg HAWAIIAN pizza

■ **Makes 4 servings**

4	**eggs**
	Salt and freshly ground pepper, to taste
1 tablespoon	**butter** (tablespoons are marked on the wrapper)
1	**thin-crust pizza shell, such as Boboli** (12-inch)
2 cups	**shredded cheddar cheese** (preshredded is available in sacks in the dairy aisle)
2	**1/4-inch-thick slices breakfast ham**
1 cup	**diced pineapple**

Preheat oven to 400°F. Beat eggs with salt and pepper. Heat a small nonstick skillet over medium heat. Melt butter in pan. Add eggs and cook, stirring, until just a little wet; remove from heat.

Put the pizza crust on a pizza pan or cookie sheet and top with scrambled eggs and lots of cheese. Cut up the ham with kitchen scissors and arrange it on the pizza. Add pineapple pieces, then place in the oven and cook until the cheese is golden and melted and the crust is crisp, 10 to 12 minutes. Cut and serve.

Breakfast or Breakfast-for-Dinner, Menu 4
Ham-and-Egg Hawaiian Pizza
Orange Freeze Shakes

Orange FREEZE Shakes

■ **Makes 4 servings**

2 cups	**orange juice**
1 pint	**orange sherbet**
6 ounces	**lemon-lime soda or seltzer** (half a can)
4 slices	**fresh orange**
	Fountain straws

Place o.j., sherbet, and soda in a blender and blend. Pour into large juice glasses to serve. Decorate glasses with a slice of fresh orange hanging on the side and a drinking straw.

Potato-and-Apple HOME FRIES

■ **Makes 4 servings**

3 tablespoons	**butter** (tablespoons are marked on the wrapper)
1 sack	**diced breakfast potatoes** (24 ounces, available on the dairy aisle)
1/2 pound	**ham steak, diced**
1	**green apple, such as Granny Smith, chopped**
1 tablespoon	**grill seasoning, such as Montreal Seasoning by McCormick or Mrs. Dash seasoning**

Place a nonstick skillet on the stove over medium-high heat. Add butter and melt it. Add potatoes, ham, and apples and season them with grill seasoning blend. Turn every 5 minutes or so, letting the potatoes brown up on all sides. Cook 20 minutes, then serve. While the potatoes cook, make the mini quiches on the next page.

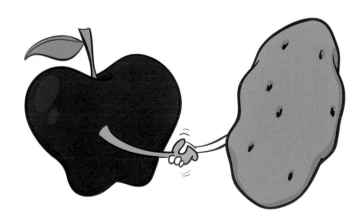

BACON-AND-CHEESE
Mini Quiches

■ **Makes 4 servings, 6 mini quiches each**

24	**filo pastry cups** (2 packages of 12; available in the frozen foods section)
4 slices	**ready-crisp bacon** (fully cooked and microwave-ready bacon)
1 cup	**shredded cheddar cheese** (preshredded is available in sacks in the dairy aisle)
2	**eggs**
A splash	**of milk**
	Salt and freshly ground pepper, to taste

Preheat oven to 375°F. Arrange the pastry cups on a cookie sheet. Cut up bacon into thin pieces with kitchen scissors. Add a little bacon to each cup. Add a sprinkle of cheese to each cup, too. Beat eggs in a bowl with a splash of milk and salt and pepper. Use a large spoon to add egg to each pastry cup to fill them up. Bake until golden, 10 to 12 minutes.

Variations: Try making the mini quiches with bits of chopped defrosted frozen broccoli and shredded cheddar cheese or chopped Canadian bacon and Swiss cheese.

Breakfast
or Breakfast-
for-Dinner,
Menu 5

Potato-and-Apple
Home Fries

Bacon-and-Cheese
Mini Quiches

JIFFY PANCAKE AND FRUIT SHORTCAKES and MAPLE SAUSAGES

■ **Makes 4 servings**

1 package	breakfast sausage patties, any brand
1/2 cup	maple syrup

BLUEBERRY SHORTCAKES

1 box	blueberry muffin mix, such as Jiffy brand
1	egg
1/3 cup	milk
	Butter or vegetable oil, for skillet or griddle
	Whipped cream
1 pint	fresh blueberries

RASPBERRY-STRAWBERRY SHORTCAKES

1 box	raspberry muffin mix, such as Jiffy brand
1	egg
1/3 cup	milk
	Butter or vegetable oil, for skillet or griddle
	Whipped cream
12	strawberries, hulled (cut off the green parts) **and sliced**

BANANA NUT AND FRUIT SHORTCAKES

1 box	banana nut muffin mix, such as Jiffy brand
1	egg
1/3 cup	milk
	Butter or vegetable oil, for skillet or griddle
	Whipped cream
1 small	banana, sliced
6	strawberries, hulled and sliced

Cook sausage patties according to package directions then use a pastry brush to brush them with maple syrup.

Make the pancakes: Heat a large nonstick skillet or griddle pan over medium heat. Mix each muffin mix in a separate bowl with egg and milk. Lightly grease skillet or griddle and pour four 3-inch blueberry pancakes onto the griddle. When bubbles appear around the edges, lift up the pancake to peek at the underside. If it looks golden brown, flip it and cook the other side. Repeat with raspberry-strawberry pancakes and then the banana nut and fruit pancakes, so you have 4 of each kind, for a total of twelve 3-inch pancakes.

Make the shortcakes: Layer a pancake with a swirl of whipped cream, a pile of fruit, then another pancake, more whipped cream and fruit, and then top with another cake. Each shortcake stack should be made with 3 small pancakes. Serve with sausage patties.

For this recipe you're using muffin mix to make pancakes to build shortcakes. Confusing, huh? But wait 'til you taste them!

REALLY BOSS BEVERAGES

AND SUPER SNACKERS!

These recipes are great at any age!

Rock on!

Cookie and Ice Cream Fill-Your-Handwiches

■ Makes 1 to as many as you need;
each pint will make 6 to 8 sammies

COOKIES
Jumbo cookies (3–4 inches), choose from:

Molasses, such as Archway brand

Pizzelles (Italian waffle cookies), **any flavor**

Jumbo chocolate-chunk cookies, such as Pepperidge Farm brand

ICE CREAM
Any flavor works, but these are my favorite combos:

For molasses cookies, use caramel swirl, vanilla, or butter pecan.

For pizzelles, use pistachio, strawberry, or Neopolitan (chocolate, vanilla, and strawberry).

For chocolate-chunk cookies, use chocolate, fudge swirl, rocky road, or vanilla.

ROLLERS
Your Fill-Your-Handwiches are great as is, or you can roll the edges in any of these cool rollers:

Mini-chocolate chips

Peanut butter chips

Chopped nuts

Toasted shredded coconut

Crushed-up toffee

Place a cookie on a plate. Take the lid off a pint of ice cream. Microwave the ice cream for 10 to 15 seconds on high to soften it for easier scooping. Scoop a HUGE scoop of ice cream on the cookie. Place another cookie on top and gently press down to make the ice cream squish out just to the edges of the cookies. Eat it this way, or roll the ice cream on the edges in some cool rollers. Can you even fit this mega-ice cream sammy in your hand?

You can make a bunch of these, too, way before dinner. Just individually wrap them up in plastic wrap and pop them into the freezer. They will keep a couple of days before they get too hard or develop that funny freezer taste.

COOKIE BITES

■ Makes as many as you like, from 1 to some; each pint will make 16 mini sammies

SMALL COOKIES

Pick your favorite—these are mine:

Chocolate-covered mint cookies, such as Girl Scout Thin Mints

Chocolate-covered mini graham cracker cookies, such as Keebler brand

Ginger snaps, any brand

Lemon snaps, any brand

Vanilla wafer cookies, such as Nilla Wafers

ICE CREAM

Your favorite flavor is always best; here are my choices for each cookie:

For chocolate-mint cookies, use mint chip or chocolate.

For chocolate-covered grahams, use rocky road or caramel swirl.

For ginger snaps, use butter pecan or vanilla.

For lemon snaps, use vanilla or strawberry.

For Nilla Wafers, use fudge ripple.

Place cookies on a plate. Take the lid off a pint of ice cream and soften it up a little in the microwave on high for 10 or 15 seconds. Use a small scoop to place balls of ice cream on the cookies. Place another cookie on top of each scoop of ice cream and press down lightly but firmly until your ice cream squishes out to the edges of the cookies. Yumm-o!

113

FUN-due Dips for Cookies, Fruit, or Cake!

■ Makes 18 to 22 chocolate-dipped cookies

FUDGE SAUCE

5 squares	**semisweet dark baking chocolate**
2 tablespoons	**unsalted butter** (tablespoons are marked on the wrapper)
2 tablespoons	**light corn syrup**
1/2 cup	**sugar**
1/2 cup	**heavy cream**
Up to 18	**shortbread cookies or 20–22 vanilla wafers**

Measure the ingredients and put them all (except for the cookies) in a small pot. Place the pot over medium-low heat or have your GH (Grown-up Helper) do it for you. Melt and stir all of the ingredients together until the sauce begins to bubble. Pour the sauce into a bowl.

Dip cookies into the sauce and eat! Try this sauce on ice cream, too, or change-up the dippers and try it with cubes of pound cake, cut-up bananas, or big strawberries.

If you're a dipper, try shortbread cookies or vanilla wafers dunked in this super fudge sauce.

CHOCOLATE DIP

■ Makes 1 cup dip

    1/4 cup   **heavy cream**
      1 cup   **semisweet chocolate chips**

Melt and stir the cream and chips in a small pot over low heat. When the chips melt, remove from heat and dip fruit, cake, or cookies in sauce.

Variations:
Butterscotch Dip, White Chocolate Dip, Peanut Dip

To make any of the variations on the chocolate dip, simply use 1 cup butterscotch, white chocolate, or peanut butter chips rather than the chocolate chips.

Ria's Double-Chips Cookies with Peanut Butter and Chocolate Chips

■ **Makes about 18 cookies**

1 + 1/4 cups	**all-purpose flour**
1/2 teaspoon	**baking soda**
	A couple of pinches salt
1/4 cup	**butter (1/2 stick), softened in the microwave for 10–15 seconds**
1/4 cup	**sugar**
1/2 cup	**honey**
1/2 cup	**semi-sweet chocolate chips**
1/2 cup	**peanut butter chips**

Preheat oven to 350°F.

Mix dry stuff (flour, baking soda, and salt) together in a big measuring cup or a small bowl. In a medium bowl, blend butter, sugar, and honey together with a rubber spatula or a mixer on low speed. Mix in the dry ingredients. Add chips and mix until everything is all creamed together and looking good. Have a taste, if you like.

Use a couple of soup spoons or tablespoons to drop blobs of the dough onto a nonstick cookie sheet. Bake till they look the color of golden brown you like, 15 to 18 minutes. Let them cool a little so the chips aren't all mushy. You can still eat them warm, if you like. Double chips are double yummy!

ABSOLUTELY *FABULOUS* 5-Minute Fudge

■ **Makes 2 pounds**

	Butter, softened, for pan
2 cups	**semisweet chocolate morsels**
1 + 1/2 cups	**butterscotch chips**
1 can	**sweetened condensed milk** (14 ounces) (save the can)
1 can	**walnut pieces** (8 ounces)
2 boxes	**raisins or golden raisins** (1 ounce each)

Grease an 8-inch cake pan with softened butter. Pour chips and sweetened condensed milk in a pot and put pot on stove over low heat Cover the empty milk can with plastic wrap. Put the can in the center of the buttered cake pan. Stir the chips and milk until they are melted together. Take the pot off the stove with the help of a GH (Grown-up Helper) and stir in the nuts and raisins. Scoop the fudge into the cake pan all around the can covered with plastic wrap so that you make a ring shape out of your fudge. Chill fudge in the fridge until it is firm. Pull the can out of the middle first, then loosen sides of fudge and bottom with a rubber spatula. Remove the fudge ring from the cake pan and cut into thin slices. Store leftover fudge in airtight container, whole or sliced.

COOKING ROCKS! PARTY POINTER

If your friends are coming over to cook up something good with you, check out this tip:

Call up your local newspaper and ask them if you can have the ends of their paper rolls. Most newspapers will be only too happy to give you these hundreds of feet of scrap paper on a roll. Cover any dining or big coffee table with long sheets from the roll and tape edges down to secure. Decorate the table by drawing on the paper with crayons or washable markers. For an easy seating idea, surround your coffee table with big pillows.

Cinnamon-Apple NACHOS

■ **Makes 4 servings**

2	**whole pita breads**
1/4 cup	**butter, melted (1/2 stick)**
3 tablespoons	**sugar**
1 teaspoon	**cinnamon**

PEANUT BUTTER SAUCE

1/2 cup	**creamy peanut butter**
1/4 cup	**whole milk**
1 tablespoon	**honey**

1	**green apple, such as Granny Smith, cored and diced**
1	**banana, halved lengthwise and sliced**

Heads up: let your GH (Grown-up Helper) do your slicing and chopping if you're not cool with your knife skills yet.

Preheat oven to 400°F.

Cut the pitas in half with kitchen scissors, so you have 2 big pockets for each pita. Cut each half into triangle shapes (4 triangles per pocket). Each triangle still has 2 layers, so separate and pull the pita bread apart at the edge where it's still attached. Place all the pita chips on a big cookie sheet. Brush melted butter onto the chips with a pastry brush. Mix sugar and cinnamon together and use your hands to sprinkle the cinnamon sugar over all the pita pieces. Bake chips until crisp and lightly browned, 5 to 7 minutes.

Meanwhile, make the peanut butter sauce: Put peanut butter, milk, and honey in a small pot. Melt together over low heat while stirring to combine the mixture. Remove sauce from heat.

Pile cinnamon-pita chips on a platter and pour the peanut sauce all over them. Top with chopped-up banana and apple and serve.

Celery Boats with Carrot Sails

LIP-SMACKING SNACKERS

■ **Makes 4 servings**

4 stalks	**celery**
2 slices	**cheese from the deli, such as cheddar, pepper-Jack, or American**
1/2 cup	**whipped cream cheese or soft herb cheese, such as Alouette**
	Sweet paprika
1 large	**carrot, peeled**

Trim a long thin strip off the round side of the celery so it sits flat. Have your GH (Grown-up Helper) do this if you are not really comfortable with your knife skills. Cut the deli cheese into 1-inch strips and line the celery stalks with the cheese strips. Fill the celery with whipped cream cheese or herb cheese, spreading it over the sliced cheese. Sprinkle the filled celery with paprika. Cut the celery stalks into 4 or 5 pieces; each piece should be a couple of inches long. These are your "boats"—now we need sails for them. The carrot needs to be thinly sliced diagonally into oval shapes. Cut each oval in half on a diagonal, too, and you'll end up with 2 triangle "sails" with rounded bottom edges. Let your GH do this slicing for you if you need help. Set your sails into each boat by pushing the rounded edge into the cheese to make the sail stand upright, then let the boats set sail straight for your mouth!

Go GREEK! Cheese Dip with Flat Bread and Veggies

■ **Makes 2 cups dip; 4 servings**

LIP-SMACKING SNACKERS

3/4 pound	**feta cheese, crumbled**
1/2 cup	**whole mllk**
1 teaspoon	**dried oregano**
1 teaspoon	**garlic powder**
	Freshly ground black pepper, to taste
1/2	**seedless English cucumber** (the long funny-looking ones), **sliced**
1 small	**red bell pepper**
1 package	**flat breads, any flavor, or 1 bag store-bought pita chips, plain or flavored**

Put the cheese, milk, and spices in a food processor. Put the top on and press go! Blend the dip until smooth. Use a rubber spatula to get the dip into a bowl. Place the bowl on a big plate so there's room to put veggies and chips with the dip. Place cucumbers on the plate in a pile. Cut the red pepper in half and pull out all the seeds and white stuff inside the pepper. Use a small knife or your kitchen scissors to cut the pepper into strips. Add the pepper strips to the plate next to the cucumbers. Add a few flat breads or a couple of handfuls of pita chips to the plate, too. Then, get dipping and snacking!

Blue Cheese Dip

LIP-SMACKING SNACKERS

■ **Makes 2 cups dip; 4 servings**

12 ounces	**blue cheese, crumbled**
1/2 cup	**white ranch dressing or buttermilk dressing**
2 tablespoons	**snipped fresh chives** (use your kitchen scissors)
2 cups	**baby carrots**
2 stalks	**celery, cut into sticks**
1 bag	**bagel chips or Melba toasts, sesame, garlic, or onion flavor**

Place cheese, ranch dressing or buttermilk, and snipped chives into a food processor. Put the lid on and turn the machine on. When the dip is smooth, take the lid off and scrape the dip into a bowl using a rubber spatula. Place the bowl on a plate and pile up carrots, celery sticks, and bagel chips or Melba toasts for dipping.

Cheesy PIZZA Popcorn

LIP-SMACKING SNACKERS

■ **Makes 4 servings**

2 tablespoons	**butter** (tablespoons are marked on the wrapper)
1 teaspoon	**garlic powder**
1 bag	**natural-flavor reduced-fat microwave popcorn, such as Newman's Own**
1 teaspoon	**dried oregano, eyeball the amount as you sprinkle it out**
1 teaspoon	**sweet paprika**
1/2 cup	**grated parmesan, Parmigiano Reggiano, or Romano cheese**

Place butter in a small microwave-safe dish and add the garlic powder. Melt the butter in the microwave for 10 to 15 seconds. Remove the butter and put the bag of popcorn in the microwave. Pop the corn according to package directions. Pour hot popped corn into a big bowl. Pour the garlic butter in a slow stream over the popcorn. Sprinkle on some oregano flakes and paprika. Add the cheese, sprinkling all over the corn. Stir the hot popcorn up with a big spoon to melt the cheese onto the corn. Taste it to adjust seasonings. It tastes a lot like pizza, right?

Mini Broccoli and Cheddar Potato Bread Melts

■ Makes 16 pieces; 4 servings

1 box	chopped frozen broccoli (10 ounces)
	Salt and freshly ground black pepper, to taste
4 slices	potato bread (available on the packaged breads aisle)
2 cups	shredded sharp cheddar cheese (available preshredded in sacks on the dairy aisle)

Defrost the broccoli by putting the whole box in a shallow, microwave-safe bowl and microwave on high for about 5 minutes. Have your GH remove the defrosted broccoli from the box—be careful of any hot steam—and place it in the middle of a clean

This snack makes a great lunch, too!

kitchen towel. Twist the towel to wring all the water out of the broccoli and into the bowl. Pour the broccoli water into the sink and wipe out the bowl. Place the dried, defrosted (but still cold) broccoli back into the bowl. Season it with salt and pepper and loosen up the pieces and spread them around the bowl. Place the bowl back into the microwave and cook the broccoli until hot, another 3 to 5 minutes.

Turn on the broiler in the big oven or the one in your toaster oven. Toast your bread. Remove the broccoli from the microwave and spread chopped broccoli evenly onto the four bread slices. Top with lots of cheese, and melt the cheese under a hot broiler. Let your GH (Grown-up Helper) do the too-hot-to-handle work for you if you are not supposed to deal with hot ovens. Place melts on a cutting board and cut each slice into 4 mini snacks.

Groovy Homemade GRANOLA

LIP-SMACKING SNACKERS

■ **Makes 6 to 7 cups granola**

3 + 1/2 cups	**oats**
2 cups	**frosted mini shredded wheat cereal, any brand**
1/4 cup	**slivered or sliced almonds** (2 ounces) (available on baking aisle)
1/4 cup	**pecan or walnut pieces** (2 ounces) (available on baking aisle)
1/4 cup	**sunflower seeds or 1/2 cup pumpkin seeds**
1/4 cup	**firmly packed brown sugar**
1/2 teaspoon	**cinnamon**
1 teaspoon	**pure vanilla extract**
1/4 cup	**vegetable oil**
12	**dried apple rings, chopped**
1/2 cup	**sweetened dried cranberries, such as Crasins by Ocean Spray**
1/2 cup	**golden raisins**

Preheat oven to 325°F.

Mix all ingredients except for the dried fruit in a bowl. Spread out the mixture on a nonstick baking sheet and bake 20 minutes. Remove from oven and transfer the granola back to the mixing bowl. Stir in the dried fruits and let the granola cool before you eat it or store it.

Mustard-Cheese Dip for PRETZELS

■ Makes 6 servings

LIP-SMACKING SNACKERS

2 tablespoons	**butter** (tablespoons are marked on the wrapper)
2 tablespoons	**all-purpose flour**
2 cups	**whole milk**
2 + 1/2 cups	**shredded cheddar cheese** (one 10-ounce sack, preshredded is available on dairy aisle)
1/2 cup	**spicy brown mustard**
1 bag	**pretzels, any shape or size** (I like Bavarian style)

Melt butter over medium-low heat in a medium saucepan. Add flour and stir into the butter; keep stirring, 1 minute, with a wire whisk. You are making a thing called roux (a French word; sounds like "roo"). By cooking flour and butter, the flour gets a nice nutty taste. Also, it allows the gluten in flour to cook and thicken the sauce. Stir the flour and butter with the whisk and add the milk at the same time. If you need extra hands, call on your GH to stir or pour. Whisk the milk into the roux until it's smooth. Let the sauce bubble and thicken, about 2 minutes. Take the sauce off the stove and add the cheese. Stir until all the cheese melts. Add the mustard and stir more to mix it in. Pour the mustard cheese into a small, microwave-safe bowl. Place the mustard-cheese dip on a plate and surround it with pretzels. If the sauce gets hard, put plastic wrap on the top of the bowl loosely and warm the dip up in the microwave for 20 seconds, then remove it with pot holders and stir it up again.

B-every-ages!

This is my collection of fun (and funny-sounding) soda fountain creations for kids of all ages. I was a fountain girl at Howard Johnson's when I was way younger than I am now. I rocked that fountain! I could make awesome orange freezes and always balance my ice cream on the rim of a fountain glass—and no one made more perfect whipped cream rosettes on their shakes! I still go to a soda fountain near my home called Papa's, in Lake Luzerne, to give myself a sweet treat in the summer months. These shakes and floats and freezes are treats indeed. They are meant to be used as desserts to a 30-Minute Meal or rewarding refreshments in honor of a special occasion, like winning a big game or a birthday party. These creations are too sweet to have everyday, for sure! Besides, if we all had treats all the time and at every meal, they wouldn't be treats, right?

Jessie's Fruit Smoothies

■ **Makes 1 MEGA-smoothie per recipe**

PEACH MELBA SMOOTHIES

1 cup	frozen sliced peaches
1/2 cup	fresh raspberries
1 cup	cold milk
1 cup	custard-style low-fat raspberry yogurt
1 cup	custard-style low-fat peach yogurt

BERRY-LICIOUS SMOOTHIES

1 cup	frozen mixed berries in juice, defrosted but still icy
1 cup	fresh strawberries, washed and hulled (cut the green part off)
1/2 cup	fresh blackberries
1/2 cup	fresh blueberries
1 cup	cold milk
1 cup	custard-style low-fat blueberry yogurt
1 cup	custard-style low-fat strawberry yogurt

STRAWBERRY-BANANA SMOOTHIES

2 cups	frozen strawberries
1 small	ripe banana, cut up
1 cup	cold milk
2 cups	custard-style low-fat strawberry-banana yogurt

TROPICAL ORANGE FREEZE SMOOTHIES

1/2 cup	frozen orange juice concentrate, defrosted just enough to scoop
1/2 cup	light coconut milk
1 cup	frozen strawberries
1 cup	fresh pineapple chunks
2 cups	custard-style low-fat vanilla yogurt

Pick a smoothie with your favorite fruits. Place ingredients into a blender and blend on high until smooth. Rock on!

Cherry-TRICKY Lime Rickey

■ **Makes 1 serving**

2 tablespoons	**lime syrup, such as Rose's Lime Juice**
1 teaspoon	**grenadine syrup or 1 tablespoon cherry juice**
	Ice
8 ounces	**cherry soda or cherry sparkling water**
1	**maraschino cherry**

Pour lime syrup and grenadine or cherry juice into a tall fountain glass. Add ice to fill the glass. Pour in cherry soda or cherry-flavored sparkling water to fill up the glass. Drop in a cherry and a straw.

Artist Unknown

Purple BURPING Cow

■ **Makes 1 serving**

1 can	**grape soda** (12 ounces)
1 scoop	**vanilla ice cream**
8	**mini marshmallows** (a small handful)

Chill a tall fountain or soda glass in the freezer, 10 minutes. Place the glass on a salad plate (smaller than a dinner plate) and get a long spoon, called a fountain spoon, and a straw. Fill the glass half full with soda. Soften the ice cream in the microwave on high for 20 seconds. Add a soft, mushy scoop of ice cream to the soda and stir until it gets mixed up. Add more soda to fill the glass and sprinkle the marshmallows on top. As you drink the soda, stir in the marshmallows then scoop them out with a spoon as you finish your soda. This is a really cool dessert to serve when your friends come over for dinner. You can have a burp contest! But please don't tell the folks that it was my idea, 'cause burps can get way outta hand and kinda gross (if they're good ones!).

Cows with spots are called Holsteins, and this drink looks like a big purple one! The burps come from the bubbles. Remember to say "Excuse me!" if some bubbles float back up to your mouth!

BRAPP.

Black-and-White-and-Red-All-Over SODA!

■ **Makes 1 serving**

2 tablespoons	**chocolate syrup**
2 tablespoons	**half-and-half or cream**
2 tablespoons	**cherry juice from maraschino cherries**
8–10 ounces	**seltzer water**
1 BIG scoop	**vanilla ice cream**
	Whipped cream in a canister
1	**maraschino cherry**

Place a tall fountain glass on a small plate. Pour chocolate syrup, half-and-half, and cherry juice into the glass and stir with a long spoon to combine. Add seltzer water to the glass to fill it up. Scoop a mega-scoop of vanilla ice cream and press it onto the edge of the fountain glass. Top it with a swirl of whipped cream and a cherry on top. When you drop the ice cream into the glass (or it falls there) get ready, because the soda will come up like a volcano and explode all over the plate! Start slurping, stirring, and eating!

What's black and white and READ all over? A newspaper! What's black and white and RED all over? This! It's a classic, really cool fountain drink.

Blue-in-the-Face FREEZE

■ **Makes 1 serving**

2 cups	**blue energy replacement drink, such as Gatorade**
2 big scoops	**lemon sorbet**
1 teaspoon	**pure vanilla extract**
A handful of	**blueberries**

Put the energy drink and sorbet into a blender and add the vanilla. Blend on high until smooth. Pour into a glass and sprinkle blueberries on top. Yumm-o!

If you've just won a big game—soccer, baseball, or basketball—you deserve a treat this good! If you've just lost, well, better luck next time and you deserve a reward even more!

WITHOUT-a-FAULT Super-Strawberry Malt

■ Makes 1 serving

1 cup	**sliced frozen strawberries, defrosted 5 minutes but still cold**
2 tablespoons	**strawberry syrup**
2 big scoops	**strawberry ice cream**
2 heaping tablespoons	**malted milk powder**
1 cup	**cold milk**
1 BIG	**fresh strawberry**

Put everything but the whole strawberry into a blender. Put the top on and blend on the highest setting until smooth. Pour into a glass. With a small knife, cut the strawberry in half up to the top but not all the way through. Place the strawberry on the edge of the glass and dip into your malt as you enjoy it. Serve with a straw.

Do you like Belgian waffles or Bosco drink mix or malted milk balls? If the answer is yes, then you like malt! This drink tastes like a strawberry-topped waffle you might get on Sundays, only you can have it any day and drink it through a straw!

Watermelon Sodas

3 cups **seedless watermelon chunks**
2 cans **lemon-lime soda or lemon-lime sparkling water**
1/4 cup **light corn syrup**
Coarse green decorating sugar (available on baking aisle)

Place watermelon in blender and puree until smooth. Add a splash of soda if the watermelon won't smush up well.

Pour the corn syrup onto a small plate and the green sugar onto another plate. Dip the rims of 4 glasses into the syrup, then into the sugar, so that the green sugar sticks all over the rim. Pour the watermelon into each glass, fill them up 1/2 or 3/4 of the way, then fill up to the top with lemon-lime soda. Add a straw to each glass and serve.

This is a super-cooling summer dessert or afternoon snack!

Chocolate-Mint HOT-and-COLD COCOA

■ **Makes 4 servings**

5 cups	**water**
4 envelopes	**instant hot cocoa mix**
1 pint	**peppermint or vanilla ice cream**
4 pieces	**peppermint stick candy or 4 candy canes**

Heat water in teakettle to boiling. Pour the cocoa powder into a teapot or coffeepot. Add the hot water or have your GH do it, carefully. Stir and combine. Place the lid on the pot. Put 1 scoop of ice cream into each of 4 mugs. Fill up with cocoa and add a peppermint stick or a candy cane to stir.

Rocky Road HOT-and-COLD COCOA

■ Makes 4 servings

5 cups	**water**
4 envelopes	**instant hot cocoa mix**
1 pint	**caramel swirl ice cream**
1 cup	**mini marshmallows**

Heat water in teakettle on the stove until it boils. Pour the cocoa powder into a teapot or coffeepot. Add the hot water or have your GH do it, carefully. Stir and combine the cocoa. Place the lid on the pot. Put 1 scoop of ice cream into each of 4 mugs. Fill up the mugs with cocoa and add a handful of mini marshmallows on top.

Put your foot

2-to-6

MAKE-YOUR-

For a real super-size 2-to-6-foot-long sub, you should have at least one other person building the sub with you. The idea is that each of you gets to build your own sub your way, then you can put your foot-long in your mouth!

Making 2-to-6-foot subs can be a really cool and fun way to make lunch or dinner if you have some friends coming over or if you and "the fam" want to make sandwich night more fun!

2-to-6-foot-long sub rolls can be ordered from most bakeries, or just buy as many 2-foot-long loaves of Italian bread as you need and line them up in a row on a LONG table.

These recipes are great at any age!

MIX-AND-MATCH
Meat and Cheese Subs
with 3 Dressings

HOW MUCH?

For each foot of sub: 1 pound meat, 1/4 pound cheese, 1/2 cup dressing, and as much veggie topping as you wish.

MEATS:

Roast turkey, smoked turkey, honey-roast turkey, turkey pastrami, roast beef, honey ham, baked ham, smoked ham, or ready-crisp bacon, crisped in microwave

CHEESES:

Muenster, cheddar, Swiss, havarti, havarti with dill

VEGGIES:

Sliced cucumber, sliced red onion, shredded lettuce, shredded carrots, sliced tomatoes

DRESSINGS:

Rachael's Russian, Dijon Mustard and Herb, Fabulous French

Rachael's Russian Dressing

■ **Makes 1 cup**

1/2 cup	**reduced-fat mayonnaise**
1/4 cup	**ketchup**
2 rounded tablespoons	**dill pickle relish or sweet red pepper relish**
1/4 small	**white onion**
	Freshly ground pepper, to taste

Mix together mayonnaise, ketchup, and relish in a small bowl. Grate the onion using a hand grater over the bowl so the juice of the onion goes into the sauce. Add a few grinds of pepper. Combine.

Dijon Mustard and Herb Dressing

■ **Makes 1 cup**

1/2 cup	**reduced-fat mayonnaise**
1/4 cup	**Dijon mustard**
1 tablespoon	**fresh lemon juice**
2 tablespoons	**chopped fresh tarragon**
2 tablespoons	**chopped fresh chives**

Mix together all the ingredients in a small bowl.

FABULOUS French Dressing

■ **Makes 1 cup**

1/3 cup	**white wine vinegar**
1/3 cup	**sugar**
1/2 cup	**ketchup**
1/2 cup	**extra-virgin olive oil (evoo)**
1/2 teaspoon	**garlic powder**
2 teaspoons	**Worcestershire sauce**
1/4 small	**white onion, finely chopped or grated**
	Salt, to taste

Put all the ingredients in a blender. Put the top in place and blend on high until dressing is combined.

MIX-AND-MATCH Italian SUPER SUBS and 2 Dressings

Mix and match whichever meats, cheeses, and dressing you like from the recipe below to make the best Italian subs ever! Mangia!

MEATS:

Genoa salami, hard salami, sliced sandwich-size pepperoni, cappicola (spicy ham), prosciutto cotto, hot sopressata, sweet sopressata

CHEESES:

Deli-sliced mild or sharp provolone, sliced mozzarella, smoked mozzarella

VEGGIES:

Chopped romaine lettuce, thinly sliced onion, sliced tomatoes

DRESSINGS:

Lemony Pepper-Parmesan, Italian Balsamic-Basil

RELISH:

2 cups giardiniera (hot vegetable salad of cauliflower, carrots, and hot peppers; available in jars in the Italian foods section of any grocery store), drained, then chopped in food processor

These recipes are great at any age, too!

Lemony Pepper-Parmesan Dressing

■ **Makes 1 cup**

3 heaping tablespoons	**mayonnaise**
	Grated zest (just the yellow part of the skin) **and juice of 1 lemon**
1 teaspoon	**freshly ground pepper, eyeball the amount** (1 teaspoon equals about 1/3 of a palmful)
3 tablespoons	**extra-virgin olive oil (evoo)** (pour to a count of 6)
1/2 cup	**grated Parmigiano Reggiano or parmesan**
Pinch of	**salt**

Combine the mayo, lemon zest, and lemon juice. To get the juice out of a lemon, heat it up in microwave for 10 seconds on high; cut the lemon in half crosswise and squeeze the lemon halves while holding them upright over the dressing bowl so that the seeds stay with the lemon halves, not in the dressing. Add pepper. Whisk the dressing and pour in the evoo while you whisk. Once the oil is combined with the lemon juice and mayo, stir in the cheese and a pinch of salt using a spoon or rubber spatula.

Italian Balsamic-Basil Dressing

■ **Makes 1 1/2 cups**

1/4 cup	**red wine vinegar**
2 tablespoons	**green salad olives with red pimiento and juice**
1 cup	**fresh basil, torn up** (20 leaves)
1/4 cup	**grated parmesan, Parmigiano Reggiano, or Romano cheese**
	Freshly ground pepper, to taste
1/2 cup to 2/3 cup	**extra-virgin olive oil (evoo), eyeball it**

Place all the ingredients in a blender. Blend on high until smooth.

Chicken and Eggplant Parm Subs

These are for the big guys, 12 and up.

Me and my bro, Manny, both love parm subs.
I like eggplant; he likes chicken. These two recipes
rock because they are much easier to make than
fried eggplant or fried chicken cutlets, and they are more
healthful, too, because the fillings are not deep-fried.
The chicken is crusted entirely in cheese— just parm,
no bread crumbs! The eggplant gets baked with garlic oil
then stacked up with smoked mozzarella cheese
and a fire-roasted tomato-basil sauce.
ROCK ON!

Chicken Parmesan Sub with Warm Tomato-Basil Veggie Salsa

■ **Makes one 1-foot sub or two 6-inch subs**

2 cups	shredded (NOT GRATED!) parmesan or Parmigiano Reggiano cheese
8 thin pieces	chicken breast cutlets
	Freshly ground pepper, to taste

SALSA:

1 small	zucchini, cut into chunks
1/2 cup	shredded carrots (a couple of handfuls) (preshredded are available in produce section)
2 cloves	garlic
2 tablespoons	extra-virgin olive oil (evoo) (2 turns of the pan)
	Salt and freshly ground pepper, to taste
2 or 3	scallions, chopped
1 can	chunky crushed or diced canned tomatoes (14 ounces)
10 leaves	fresh basil, chopped or torn
	Crusty sub rolls (one foot of sub roll or two 6-inch rolls)

Heat a nonstick skillet over medium to medium-high heat. Pour the cheese into a shallow dish and press chicken into the cheese on both sides, gently coating with cheese. Place 4 cutlets at a time into a hot pan and cook until the cheese turns brown before turning, 3 or 4 minutes. Season the chicken with a little pepper. Cook until both sides are golden, remove cutlets, and cover with loose foil to keep warm. Repeat with remaining cutlets.

While chicken cooks, start the salsa: Put zucchini, carrots, and garlic in a food processor and press pulse several times to chop veggies into small bits.

Remove the last batch of chicken, keeping the foil on it to retain the heat. To the same skillet, add evoo, then add the zucchini, carrots, and garlic. Season with salt and pepper and sauté 2 or 3 minutes. Add scallions and tomatoes and cook another minute or 2 to heat through. Remove warm salsa from heat and stir in lots of basil. Place chicken on bread and layer it with veggie salsa. Mangia, baby, mangia!

HEADS UP: Parm is short for parmesan, which is the American version of a special Italian cheese, Parmigiano Reggiano. Parmigiano has a better, sweeter, and nuttier flavor than parmesan, but it can be expensive, too. On the other hand, when it's grated up, either parm, domestic (from the U.S.) or imported (from Italy), goes a long way!

ROASTED EGGPLANT with Fire-Roasted Tomato Sauce, Smoked Mozzarella, and Parmesan

■ **Makes one 1-foot sub or two 6-inch subs**

1/2 cup	**extra-virgin olive oil (evoo), eyeball it**
2 large cloves	**garlic, cracked away from skins**
1 medium to large	**firm eggplant**
	Salt and freshly ground pepper, to taste
1/2	**red onion, chopped**
1 can	**chopped fire-roasted tomatoes, such as Muir Glen brand (14 ounces)**
1 small can	**tomato sauce** (8 ounces)
1/2 pound	**smoked mozzarella, thinly sliced**
	Crusty sub rolls (one foot of sub roll or two 6-inch rolls)
1/2 cup	**shredded Parmigiano Reggiano cheese**
10	**fresh basil leaves, thinly sliced or torn**

Preheat oven to 450°F.

Put the evoo in a small microwave-safe dish and add garlic; microwave on high for 15 to 20 seconds. Let stand.

Trim ends off eggplant; slice off a sliver from one side, so the eggplant sits flat for you to slice it. Cut the eggplant into 1/2-inch-thick slices. Arrange the eggplant on cookie sheets.

Get the evoo from the microwave. Using a pastry brush, lightly brush both sides of sliced eggplant with garlic oil. Season eggplant with salt and pepper and roast in hot oven until tender, about 15 minutes, flipping eggplant once.

Meanwhile, pull garlic cloves out of evoo and chop. Take the remaining evoo and place in a skillet over medium heat. Add garlic and onion. Sauté 2 to 3 minutes, then stir in tomatoes and tomato sauce; season with salt and pepper. Lower heat and allow sauce to thicken.

When eggplant is done, remove it from the oven. Place sliced mozzarella on the bottom of sub roll. Pile layers of hot cooked eggplant on top. Cover eggplant with parm cheese, then tomato sauce. Garnish with basil, and open wide—it's time to belly up!

IMPORTANT:
Whether you use parmesan or Parmigiano Reggiano, use shredded cheese for these recipes, not grated. Grated cheese will be too small to make the crust on the chicken.

SECTION 3

Recipes for ages

12

Spinach and Mushroom LASAGNA ROLL-UPS

with Gorgonzola Cream Sauce, Steamed Lemon-Scented Asparagus, and Broiled Tomatoes

■ **Makes 4 servings**

	Salt and freshly ground pepper, to taste
8	curly-edge lasagna noodles
1 + 1/2 pounds	fresh asparagus
1	lemon
2 tablespoons	extra-virgin olive oil (evoo) (2 turns of the pan), **plus more for drizzling**
16	crimini (baby portobello) mushroom caps, cleaned with a damp towel and finely chopped in food processor
1 small	yellow onion, finely chopped
2 cloves	garlic, minced
4	vine-ripened tomatoes
1 box	frozen chopped spinach, defrosted and squeezed dry in a clean towel (10 ounces)
1/4 teaspoon	ground nutmeg, eyeball the amount
2 cups	ricotta cheese
1 cup	chicken stock
1/2 cup	heavy cream (3 turns of the pan)
8 ounces	gorgonzola cheese, crumbled

Bring a large pot of water to a boil for the lasagna. You're going to put a colander over (not in!) the water to steam the asparagus in, so be sure to leave enough room at the top of the pot. When the water boils, add salt, then noodles. Cook noodles to almost tender,

or al dente, 12 to 14 minutes. Drain.

While pasta is cooking, prepare the asparagus: Hold a piece of asparagus at both ends and push the ends together, making the spear snap and break. Where the asparagus snaps becomes your guide for trimming off the tough ends of the rest of the asparagus. Trim the spears (discarding the ends) and place them in a small colander. Pull 2 big pieces of peel off the lemon and add them to the asparagus. At least 4 or 5 minutes before the pasta is done, place the colander over the boiling water in the pasta pot; place a lid on the colander and steam asparagus until the tips are just tender, about 4 minutes. Place the asparagus on a plate. Cut the lemon in half and squeeze the juice from 1/2 lemon over the asparagus (squeeze it right side up so the seeds don't fall into the asparagus); add a little salt. Serve at room temperature.

In a medium skillet over medium heat, warm 2 tablespoons evoo then add mushrooms, onions, and garlic. Season with salt and

My First Menu

Spinach and Mushroom
Lasagna Roll-ups with
Gorgonzola Cream Sauce

Steamed Lemon-Scented
Asparagus

Broiled Tomatoes

pepper and cook until mushrooms give off their juices and darken and onions are tender, 7 or 8 minutes.

While the vegetables cook, prepare the tomatoes: Split tomatoes lengthwise and arrange on a small baking dish. Drizzle with evoo and season with salt and pepper. Place a rack in the top position in the oven and preheat the broiler.

Add chopped spinach to the pan with the mushrooms and heat through for 1 minute. Add salt, pepper, and nutmeg (your secret ingredient!). Add ricotta cheese and stir into mixture to heat cheese through, 1 minute. Remove pan from heat but leave mixture in the warm skillet.

Make the sauce: Heat chicken stock and cream in a small pot over medium heat until liquid bubbles, then melt gorgonzola cheese into the liquid and return it to a bubble. Simmer sauce on low heat.

Broil tomatoes, 2 minutes. Place on a serving plate.

Place cooked lasagna noodles on a large work surface or cutting board. Cool 1 minute to handle, but work while pasta is still warm. Spread each lasagna noodle with a layer of spinach-mushroom filling. Place half the gorgonzola cheese sauce into a serving dish. Roll up pasta and arrange the 8 bundles in the dish. Dot the bundles with remaining spoonfuls of the cheese sauce and serve. Serve with steamed asparagus and broiled tomatoes.

Tomato, Basil, and Cheese BAKED PASTA

■ Makes 4 to 6 servings

1 pound	**medium shell pasta**
3 large cloves	**garlic, skins on**
2 tablespoons	**extra-virgin olive oil (evoo)** (2 turns of the pan)
1/2	**small to medium yellow onion**
1 can	**crushed San Marzano or other Italian tomatoes, any brand** (28 ounces)
1/2 cup	**fresh basil, torn into small pieces** (10–12 leaves)
	Salt and freshly ground black pepper, to taste
1 cup	**store-bought basil pesto sauce**
1 cup	**ricotta cheese**
1/2 cup	**grated parmesan or Parmigiano Reggiano cheese** (a couple of handfuls)
1/2 pound	**fresh mozzarella cheese, shredded**

Bring a large pot of water to a boil and salt the water. Add pasta and cook for a minute or two less time than package directions say. The pasta will soak up more juice and keep on cooking after we drain it, so we need it to be a little under-cooked. The shells will proba-bly cook for 9 or 10 minutes.

Preheat a big, deep skillet or a medium saucepan over medium heat.

First (on next)
Dinner Date Menu

Tomato, Basil,
and Cheese
Baked Pasta

Lemony
Pepper-Parmesan
Dressed Salad

Place garlic on a cutting board and place the flat of your knife on top of each clove. Carefully give the garlic a whack with the palm of your hand to separate the cloves from the skins. Throw out the skins and chop up the garlic. Remember to keep your fingers curled under and the edge of your knife tilted slightly away from your body.

Add evoo by pouring a slow stream of it twice around the pan. This will be about 2 tablespoons, just enough to coat the bottom of the pan. Do not let the oil pour out too fast; you want a slow, steady stream. Add the garlic to the oil. To chop the onion, cut the ends off and cut the whole onion down the center. Wrap half and save it for another use. Cut the other half into thin slices then turn the slices a quarter turn and chop them again. Hold the tip of the knife on the cutting board and lift the back of the knife up and down over the onion to make the pieces really small. Add the chopped-up onion to the garlic and oil. Cook, stirring a lot, until the onions are mushy and look cooked, about 5 minutes.

Add the tomatoes to the onions and stir. When the tomatoes come to a bubble, reduce the heat under the sauce to low. Stir in basil pieces to wilt them. Season the sauce with salt and pepper.

Preheat the broiler to high and place a rack in the center of the oven.

Drain pasta shells. Add them to a casserole dish. Add pesto sauce, ricotta cheese, and a handful of grated parmesan. Stir carefully and coat the hot pasta with the pesto and cheeses. Pour the hot tomato and basil sauce over the pasta, as much as you like. You can always serve a little extra at the table. Scatter the mozzarella cheese over the pasta. Add a final sprinkle of parmesan as well. Place the casserole under the broiler in the middle of oven, 10 to 12 inches from the heat. Let the cheese melt and bubble on top, 3 to 5 minutes.

COOKING ROCKS! DATE NIGHT TIP

Having a date night at home is cool because cooking for someone is really original. Hanging out in the mall or a restaurant is boring and can be expensive. Movies are cool, but you can watch one at home, too, after your dinner. Besides, your parents will like it because they'll know where you are and if they leave you alone, they can have the leftovers! Ladies, it's an old saying, but it's true: the way to a guy's heart is through his stomach. And guys, if you really want to impress a girl, try cooking for her!

Lemony Pepper-Parmesan Dressed Salad

■ **Makes 4 servings**

	Grated zest and juice of 1 lemon
3 heaping tablespoons	**mayonnaise**
1 teaspoon	**freshly ground black pepper, eyeball the amount (1 teaspoon equals about 1/3 of a palmful)**
3 tablespoons	**extra-virgin olive oil (evoo)**
1/2 cup	**grated Parmigiano-Reggiano cheese**
	Pinch of salt
2 hearts of	**romaine lettuce**

Use the small holes of a cheese grater to grate the zest of the lemon (that's the yellow part of the skin—not the white part). Squeeze the juice from the lemon. (To get the juice out of a lemon, heat it up in microwave for 10 seconds on high. Cut the lemon in half crosswise. Squeeze the lemon halves while holding them upright over the dressing bowl so that the seeds stay in the lemon halves, not in the dressing.)

Combine the mayo, lemon zest, and lemon juice in a bowl. Add pepper to the dressing bowl, too. Whisk the dressing and pour in the evoo while you whisk. If you pour in a slow, steady stream, 3 tablespoons of evoo will pour out in a count to 6. Once the oil is combined with the lemon juice and the mayonnaise, you can switch utensils and stir in the cheese and salt with a spoon or rubber spatula.

Chop up the lettuce into 2-inch pieces. Place the lettuce in a salad bowl and top with the dressing when you are ready to serve dinner.

I wrote this menu for my good friend Camille. She's blonde, gorgeous, and 15. She dates, but mostly likes hanging out with friends. She says this meal is cool for her friends that are into sports because it has a lot of carbs. Also, it combines her favorites: pesto and pasta and red sauce, too!

Mediterranean Chicken and Pasta Toss

■ **Makes 4 servings**

	Salt and freshly ground pepper, to taste
1 pound	**penne rigate pasta**
2 tablespoons	**extra-virgin olive oil (evoo)** (2 turns of the pan)
1 pound	**chicken tenders or chicken breast, cut into bite-size pieces**
2 tablespoons	**butter** (tablespoons are marked on the wrapper)
12–16 medium	**white mushrooms, chopped**
1/2 cup	**pitted kalamata olives or other black olives, chopped**
1 can	**quartered artichoke hearts in water, drained** (14 ounces)
1 box	**frozen chopped broccoli or frozen chopped spinach, defrosted in microwave**
	Blender Caesar Lite Dressing or 1 cup store-bought Caesar salad dressing, such as Ken's Steak House Lite Caesar
	Grated Romano cheese, to pass at table

BLENDER CAESAR LITE DRESSING

3 tablespoons	**anchovy paste**
1 large clove	**garlic, cracked away from skin** (whack with knife or pan)
	Juice of 1 lemon
A few drops	**Worcestershire sauce**
1/2 cup	**grated Romano cheese**
1 teaspoon	**freshly ground pepper**
1/4 cup	**extra-virgin olive oil (evoo)** (pour to the count of 5)

Put a large pot of water on the stove to boil for pasta. When the water boils, salt it and add the pasta. Cook the pasta to al dente, which means "to the bite"—not too mushy.

Heat a big skillet over medium-high heat. Add evoo and chicken and lightly brown chicken evenly all over, 2 to 3 minutes. Do not move the chicken before it's ready; the meat will stick to the pan until it cooks a little. Carefully transfer the chicken to a plate and return the skillet to the stovetop. Reduce heat to medium. Add butter; add mushrooms and season them with salt and pepper. Cook mushrooms until they become tender and darken a little, 3 to 5 minutes. Add olives and artichokes to the skillet and let them warm through. Drain defrosted broccoli or spinach in a clean kitchen towel. Wrap the towel around the defrosted veggies and twist to get all of the liquid out. Separate the drained broccoli or spinach with your fingers as you add it to the skillet. Season the mixture with salt and pepper and adjust to your taste. Add the chicken back to the skillet.

If you are preparing homemade dressing, blend all the ingredients together in the blender.

Carefully drain cooked pasta, asking for help from a GH (Grown-up Helper) if the pot is too much for you to handle. Add the pasta to the veggies and stir together with Caesar dressing. Eat hot or cold.

My sister, Maria, makes this meal for my niece and nephew. I love it because you can eat it hot or cold, depending on the weather outside. Plus, leftovers never have to be reheated!

Italian Flag Sundaes!

■ **Makes 4 sundaes**

1 pint	**pistachio ice cream**
1 pint	**vanilla ice cream**
2 cups	**frozen sliced strawberries in syrup, defrosted**
	Whipped cream in spray canister
1 bar	**dark chocolate**
	Wafer cookies, chocolate or vanilla

Place one large scoop of pistachio ice cream and one of vanilla in each of 4 dessert bowls. Top with strawberries and a swirl of whipped cream. Using a vegetable peeler, peel curls of chocolate off the side of a dark chocolate bar; finish the sundaes with chocolate curls and serve with wafer cookies for dipping and crunching.

Hot -or- Cold menu

Mediterranean Chicken and Pasta Toss

Italian Flag Sundaes

FISH-IN-A-SACK

■ Makes 4 servings

4	**brown paper grocery sacks**
2	**zucchini**
4	**scallions, chopped or snipped with kitchen scissors into 1-inch pieces**
1 cup	**shredded carrots** (preshredded are available in produce department)
1 pint	**cherry or grape tomatoes**
	Salt and freshly ground pepper, to taste
1/2 cup	**fresh flat-leaf parsley, chopped or snipped**
2 to 2 + 1/2 pounds	**fresh cod, cut into 4 portions**
1	**lemon, very thinly sliced**
1/4 cup	**extra-virgin olive oil (evoo)**

Preheat oven to 375°F.

Cut each sack in half across, making shorter paper bags; discard the tops. Open the bags up and place 2 bags on each of 2 cookie sheets or baking sheets.

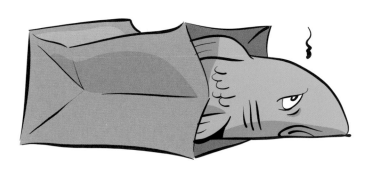

Cut a thin slice off of the length of one side of each zucchini (this will make it more stable for you to cut the zucchini); slice them into 1/4-inch-thick disks. Arrange a layer of about 8 disks in the bottom of each sack, like rows of dominoes that have fallen.

Scatter a couple of handfuls of scallions, a few tablespoons of shredded carrots, and some whole tomatoes over the zucchini in each bag. Try to keep the amounts even. Season the veggies with salt and pepper as you are working. Add the parsley to the veggies, about 2 tablespoons per sack. Season the fish with salt and pepper and arrange each portion directly on top of the veggies in each sack. Cover the fish with thin slices of lemon. Drizzle about 1 tablespoon evoo down over each portion of fish and veggies. Seal the bags by rolling them tightly—but stop rolling an inch or so above the fish. Bake 20 minutes. Place a whole sack on each plate and serve. Cut sacks open at the dinner table to reveal the cooked fish and veggies. Who knew eating out of a sack could be so fancy!

Brown Bag It

Fish-in-a-Sack

Fancy Fruit and Cake Cups

Fancy Fruit + Cake Cups

■ **Makes 6 cake cups (Someone always has seconds!)**

6	**individual sponge cakes** (3-inch)
6 tablespoons	**raspberry all-fruit spread**
3	**individual-portion cups prepared vanilla pudding** (4-ounce) (available in the dairy case)
1	**kiwi**
1/2 pint	**fresh raspberries**

Place sponge cakes on a serving platter. Spread 1 tablespoon raspberry spread into each cake cup and top with 1/2 serving vanilla pudding, about 1/4 cup pudding per serving.

Using a small knife, cut the ends off the kiwi and stand it upright. Cut off strips of the skin with the knife, working from top to bottom. Slice peeled kiwi into 6 disks. Top each filled cake cup with a kiwi slice. Arrange raspberries around the sliced kiwis in each cup and serve.

Presto! Pasta and Pesto Salad

■ **Makes 8 side dish servings or 4 entrée servings**

1 pound	**medium pasta shells or penne rigate**
1 tub	**store-bought pesto** (1+1/2 cups, available on the dairy aisle)
	Grated zest (just the yellow part of the skin) **and juice of 1 lemon**
2	**scallions, chopped or snipped with kitchen scissors**
1/2 pint	**grape tomatoes, halve some of them and leave some whole**
1 tub (1 pound)	**bocconcini** (bite-size pieces of fresh mozzarella cheese), **halved, or a 1-pound ball of fresh mozzarella, diced**
1 cup	**fresh basil leaves**
	Salt and freshly ground pepper, to taste

COLD MENU FOR HOT NIGHTS

presto! pasta and pesto salad

shrimp or chicken lettuce wraps with creamy caesar dressing

Cook pasta according to package directions to al dente (with a "bite" to it, or slightly chewy). Drain pasta and run under cold water. This cold shock will stop the cooking process and cool the pasta for the salad. Drain the pasta again when it is cool. Get all the water off with a vigorous shake, or your salad will be wet.

Place pesto in a large bowl. Add lemon zest and lemon juice. Add scallions, tomatoes, and cheese to the bowl, then the pasta. Stir salad up from the bottom and coat it evenly with the pesto. Season with salt and pepper. Tear basil leaves into strips, add them to the salad, and fold them in.

To take the salad on a picnic, pack it in large plastic food-storage bags. Take paper bowls and plastic forks to serve. When you're ready, pour the salad out of the sacks into the bowls—no serving utensils required, plus the remaining salad is ready to go back in the fridge when you get back home.

Caprese is a salad of sliced tomatoes layered with sliced fresh mozzarella cheese and basil leaves. This pasta salad incorporates all three of those elements. Also, the salad is the color of the Italian flag: red, white, and green!

It's picnic-perfect, too, in that it travels well and can be eaten at room temperature because it has no mayonnaise in it.

Shrimp or Chicken Lettuce Wraps with Creamy Caesar Dressing

■ Makes 4 servings

2 hearts of	**romaine lettuce**
1 pound	**fully cooked jumbo shrimp** (available at the fish counter)
1	**rotisserie chicken** (available near the deli or meat section)
3 heaping tablespoons	**reduced-fat mayonnaise**
1 clove	**garlic, crushed**
	Grated zest (just the yellow part of the skin) **and juice of 1 lemon**
2 tablespoons	**anchovy paste** (optional, but it tastes better with it in—if you think you don't like anchovies, try them in this sauce; they just taste salty and yummy!)
1/2 cup	**grated Parmigiano Reggiano or parmesan cheese** (a few handfuls)
2 teaspoons	**Worcestershire sauce, eyeball it**
1 teaspoon	**freshly ground pepper, eyeball the amount** (1 teaspoon equals about 1/3 of a palmful)
3 tablespoons	**extra-virgin olive oil (evoo)** (pour to the count of 4)

Cut bottoms off the romaine and cut the heads in half lengthwise. Separate and wash the leaves. Let them dry in the dish rack while you prepare the rest of the menu.

Remove the tails from the shrimp and place the shrimp in a bowl, or if this is a picnic meal, pack for travel.

Cut the breast meat off the chicken, then cut the legs and thighs off using kitchen scissors. Slice the meat up on an angle and arrange on a plate or in a plastic container.

Make the dressing: Place mayo, garlic, lemon zest and juice, anchovy paste (if using), cheese, Worcestershire, and pepper in a blender and turn it on. Stream the evoo into the dressing through center of the lid. When the oil is combined, remove the thick dressing with a spatula to a bowl or a portable plastic container.

Place lettuce on a serving platter or pack in large plastic bag or container to travel.

To assemble, spread a little dressing onto a lettuce leaf. Fill leaf with a large shrimp or sliced cold chicken. Fold lettuce up around meat, like a lettuce taco, and eat.

This recipe requires no cooking and is served cold, so it makes a perfect picnic in the hot summer months!

ANTIPA-STICKS

■ **Makes 12 sticks, 4 to 6 servings**

12	**marinated mushrooms**
12 pieces	**marinated artichoke**
12 strips	**1-inch wide roasted red pepper**
12 small	**pepperoncini** (light green, hot peppers) (optional)
1 slab	**1-inch thick provolone cheese, cut into 12 cubes**
1 slab	**1-inch thick Genoa salami from the deli, cubed into 12 bite-size pieces**
12	**bamboo skewers** (8-inch)

Make an assembly line of all the ingredients by lining them up in piles in a row on a work surface. The red pepper strips should be rolled up so they can fit on the stick. Stack the sticks in this order: mushroom, artichoke, rolled red pepper strip, pepperoncini (if desired), cheese, salami. Serve, or pack up for a picnic or a tailgate party in large food storage bags.

Marinated mushrooms and artichoke hearts, roasted red peppers, and hot peppers are all available on the Italian foods aisle in glass jars.

Chunks of provolone cheese are available in the specialty cheese case of the market, or you can get a large piece at the deli.

Stacked PANINI* Sticks

■ **Makes 6 servings**

6	**round crusty rolls** (plain Kaisers will do if your store offers no others)
1 pound	**spreadable cheese, such as Robiola** (Italian cheese) **or Alouette brand garlic and herb cheese**
1/2 pound	**prosciutto di Parma** (Italian ham, available at deli or in presliced imported packages near deli case)
2 cups	**arugula, well washed**
6	**bamboo skewers** (8-inch)

Split rolls and spread the bottom half of each roll with cheese. Top with a few pieces of arugula and 2 thin slices ham; set the top in place and press down. Cut into quarters or grill to toast the roll, then cut. Stack the four quarters of each sandwich on a stick. Serve or pack the stacked sticks into large food-storage bags.

In Italy, my favorite panino (sandwich) is made with ham (prosciutto di Parma), cheese (Robiola), and arugula (rucola or rocket—spicy, dark green lettuce). You can eat it cold, or press it and grill it on a sandwich press or in a skillet. To press it in a skillet, put a heavy skillet on top of the sandwich as it cooks over medium heat.

Rachael

ITA
PAR

BOO
MY HOU
New Yo
U.S.A

Stacked CAPRESE Sticks

■ **Makes 6 servings**

12 **bamboo skewers** (8-inch)
12 **grape tomatoes**
12 **basil leaves**
12 **bocconcini** (bite-size pieces of fresh mozzarella; available in tubs near Italian cheeses)
   Extra-virgin olive oil (evoo), for drizzling
   Salt and freshly ground pepper, to taste

On each skewer, place a grape tomato, a folded basil leaf, and 1 piece of bocconcino. Drizzle the sticks with evoo, salt, and pepper. Pack for a picnic in plastic food-storage bags or serve as is.

Italian Supper on a Stick:

Antipa-sticks
(antipasti on a stick)

Stacked Panini Sticks
(sandwich bites on a stick)

Stacked FRUiT Sticks

■ **Makes 6 servings**

1 **cored fresh pineapple** (available in sacks or tubs in the produce department)

2 **seedless navel oranges**

6 large **strawberries, hulled** (remove the greens with a small paring knife)

6 **bamboo skewers** (8-inch)

Cut pineapple lengthwise into 4 pieces. Cut each wedge into 6 chunks, making 24 pieces. Trim the ends off oranges, leaving the peel on the rest of the orange. Cut each orange into 6 wedges then cut wedges in half crosswise. Stack 4 pieces each pineapple and orange wedges on the sticks and mix in one large strawberry per skewer in the middle. When you eat the sticks, bite the oranges off the peels and discard peels. Serve skewers on a platter or place in plastic food-storage sacks to take on a picnic.

Stacked Fruit Sticks

Stacked Caprese Sticks
(tomato, basil, and mozzarella sticks)

Spicy Shrimp Burgers

■ **Makes 4 burgers**

1 pound	**raw small salad shrimp**
1 small stalk	**celery, from the heart**
1/2 small	**yellow onion, cut into chunks**
1/2 small	**green bell pepper, seeded and cut into pieces**
1 clove	**garlic**
A handful of	**fresh flat-leaf parsley leaves**
1 tablespoon	**Old Bay seasoning** (available near fish department)
1/2 teaspoon	**cayenne pepper**
1 teaspoon	**chili powder**
	Grated zest (just the yellow part of the skin) **of 1 lemon**
	Salt and freshly ground black pepper, to taste
2 tablespoons	**extra-virgin olive oil (evoo)** (2 turns of the pan)
4	**English muffins, sandwich-size plain or sourdough flavor, such as Thomas' brand**
1/4 cup	**mayonnaise**
1/4 cup	**chili sauce, salsa, or taco sauce**
	Boston lettuce leaves

Put half the shrimp into a food processor and grind them up. Transfer the ground shrimp to a bowl using a rubber spatula. Add the remaining whole shrimp to the bowl. Put the empty food processor bowl back in place and add celery, onion, bell pepper, garlic, and parsley; pulse-grind the mixture into a fine chop. Add the vegetable mixture to the shrimp. Add Old Bay seasoning, cayenne, chili powder, lemon zest, salt, and pepper to the bowl. Stir the shrimp mixture to combine.

Preheat a large nonstick skillet over medium to medium-high heat. Add evoo. Use a large metal ice cream scoop to scoop 4 mounds of shrimp-burger mixture into the pan. Gently pat down to form patties. Fry patties until they firm up and the shrimp turn whitish-pink, 3 to 5 minutes on each side.

Split and toast the English muffins. Mix mayo and chili sauce together. Place burgers on muffin bottoms and top with lettuce. Slather the top of the muffins with sauce and set in place.

Salt and Vinegar and Cayenne FRIES

■ **Makes 4 servings**

1 sack	**frozen extra-crispy French fries** (1 pound)
2 teaspoons	**fine salt**
1 teaspoon	**cayenne pepper**
	White, malt, or cider vinegar, for sprinkling

Cook fries according to package directions. Combine salt and cayenne. When fries are done, remove from oven and toss with spicy salt, seasoning to your taste. Sprinkle with vinegar and serve immediately.

Whenever you use cayenne pepper, wash your hands with soap right away and NEVER touch your eyes before you do or WOW will it sting and burn and make you cry, a lot.

CAJUN CRUDITÉS

■ **Makes 4 servings**

2 large	**carrots, peeled and thinly sliced on an angle**
1/2	**seedless English cucumber** (super long and wrapped in plastic), **thinly sliced on an angle into ovals**
4 small stalks	**celery from the heart, cut into 4-inch pieces**
1/2	**green bell pepper, cut into thin strips**
	Juice of 1 lime
	Salt, to taste
1	**teaspoon chili powder**

Arrange sliced veggies on a platter and squeeze lime juice over them. Season vegetables with salt and chili powder to taste then serve.

Southern Spice
Menu

Spicy Shrimp
Burgers

Salt and Vinegar
and Cayenne Fries

Cajun Crudités

Mexican Deep-Dish Pan Pizza

MEXICAN MEAT-ZZA

■ **Makes 4 servings**

2 boxes	**corn muffin mix, such as Jiffy brand** (8 + 1/2 ounces each)
2	**eggs**
4 tablespoons	**butter, melted** (1/2 stick)
1 + 1/2 cups	**whole milk**
	Extra-virgin olive oil (evoo) or vegetable oil, for pan
1 cup	**frozen corn kernels**

TOPPING:

1 tablespoon	**extra-virgin olive oil (evoo) or vegetable oil** (1 turn of the pan)
1 pound	**ground beef**
1 small	**yellow onion, finely chopped**
2 teaspoons	**ground cumin**
1 tablespoon	**chili powder** (1 palmful)
2 teaspoons	**cayenne pepper sauce, such as Frank's Red Hot**
	Salt, to taste
2 + 1/2 cups	**shredded cheddar or Jack cheese** (one 10-ounce sack, preshredded is available on the dairy aisle)
1/2	**red bell pepper, chopped**
1 small can	**sliced chiles or jalapeños** (2 + 1/4 ounces), **drained**
2	**scallions, chopped**
2	**small vine-ripened tomatoes, seeded and diced**
2	**tablespoons drained sliced green olives** (salad olives)
1–2 tablespoons	**chopped fresh cilantro, for garnish** (optional)
1 cup	**mild to medium taco sauce, to pass at table**

Preheat oven to 400°F.

Mix together 2 packages muffin mix with eggs, melted butter, and milk. Then, stir in the corn. Wipe a large, oven-safe (double-wrap the handle in aluminum foil if it's plastic) nonstick skillet with a little oil and pour in the muffin mix. Place pan in oven and bake in center of the oven until cornbread is light golden in color, 12 to 15 minutes.

Place a second skillet over medium-high heat and add a little oil. Add beef and cook until brown, breaking it up and stirring it as it cooks. Add onions, cumin, chili powder, cayenne sauce, and salt, and cook meat 5 minutes more.

Remove cornbread from oven (don't turn it off yet) and top with meat, cheese, red bell pepper, chiles, scallions, tomatoes, and olives. Put pan back in oven and cook 5 minutes more to melt cheese. Garnish with cilantro, if desired. Cut into 8 wedges and serve from the skillet. Pass taco sauce at the table to sprinkle on top.

Barbecued Chicken PIZZAS!

PIZZA! PIZZA!

■ **Makes 4 servings**

1	**store-bought pizza crust, such as Boboli brand** (12-inch)
1/2 cup	**barbecue sauce, any brand**
2 cups	**chopped cooked chicken, such as rotisserie chicken or leftover roast chicken**
2 + 1/2 cups	**shredded cheddar cheese** (one 10-ounce sack, preshredded is available on the dairy aisle)
2	**scallions, chopped**
1/2 small	**red bell pepper, chopped**

Preheat oven to 400°F.

Put the pizza crust on a pizza tray or large cookie sheet. Cover with barbecue sauce, as you would pizza sauce. Top with chicken, cheese, and veggies and bake until golden and bubbly on top, 12 to 15 minutes. Cut into 8 pieces and serve.

3 Groovy New Pies to Make in Minutes—Take Your Pick!

Pesto, Spinach, and Broccoli Pizza!

PIZZA! PIZZA!

■ **Makes 4 servings**

1 box	**frozen chopped spinach** (10 ounces)
1 box	**frozen chopped broccoli** (10 ounces)
1	**store-bought pizza crust, such as Boboli brand** (12-inch)
1 cup	**store-bought pesto sauce, such as Contadina brand** (available on the dairy aisle)
2 + 1/2 cups	**shredded mozzarella cheese or Italian 4-cheese blend** (one 10-ounce sack, preshredded is available on dairy aisle)
2 cloves	**garlic, minced**

Preheat oven to 375°F.

Defrost spinach in microwave, 5 minutes on high. Place spinach in a clean kitchen towel and wring the spinach dry; reserve in a small bowl. Repeat process with the broccoli, and add to spinach.

Place the pizza crust on a pizza pan or a cookie sheet and spread basil pesto sauce over the crust. Top with spinach, broccoli, and cheese. Sprinkle garlic on top and put it in the oven. Bake until bubbly and lightly browned on top, 15 to 18 minutes. Cut into 8 slices and serve.

Breakfast Hawaiian PIZZA with Ham, Eggs, Cheese, and Pineapple

PIZZA! PIZZA!

■ **Makes 4 servings**

2 tablespoons	**extra-virgin olive oil (evoo) (2 turns of the pan)**
1/2 pound	**breakfast ham, chopped**
6 large	**eggs, beaten**
	Salt and freshly ground pepper, to taste
1	**store-bought pizza crust, such as Boboli brand (12-inch)**
2 & 1/2 cups	**shredded cheddar cheese (one 10-ounce sack, preshredded is available on the dairy aisle)**
1/2	**fresh cored pineapple, diced**

Preheat oven to 400°F.

Heat a nonstick skillet over medium to medium-high heat. Add evoo. Add ham and cook 2 minutes. Beat eggs with salt and pepper. Add to ham, and scramble (cook, stirring, until no longer runny).

Place the pizza on a pizza pan or cookie sheet. Top with scrambled eggs, ham, cheese, and pineapple. Bake until crust is crisp and cheese is bubbly, 12 to 15 minutes. Cut into 8 pieces and serve.

Eat this one morning, noon, or night!

Thai Seafood Salad & Lettuce Wraps!

■ **Makes 4 servings**

1 pound	**small cooked shrimp, tails removed**
1 tub	**lump crabmeat (6 ounces)** (available in the fish department)
1	**red bell pepper, seeded and thinly sliced**
4	**scallions, chopped on an angle into 1-inch pieces**
1 cup	**basil leaves, shredded or torn**
1 tablespoon	**hot sauce, Asian or Tabasco**
Juice of 2	**limes**
1 teaspoon	**sugar**
1 teaspoon	**salt**
2 tablespoons	**vegetable oil**
1 head	**Bibb or Boston lettuce or 1/2 head iceberg lettuce, leaves separated**

In a bowl, combine shrimp, crabmeat, red bell pepper, scallions, and basil.

Make the dressing: In a small bowl, combine hot sauce, lime juice, sugar, salt, and oil. Pour the dressing over the salad and adjust seasoning, adding more hot sauce or salt, to taste. To serve, pile the seafood salad in lettuce leaves, wrapping leaves up and around the salad as you eat.

MAKE YOUR OWN TAKE-OUT

Cold Soy-Sesame Noodles and Spring Rolls

■ **Makes 4 servings**

1 package	**frozen store-bought spring rolls, vegetable, pork, or shrimp**
1/2 cup	**plum sauce or duck sauce**
2 tablespoons	**tamari** (dark soy sauce)
2 teaspoons	**dark sesame oil**
1 teaspoon	**red-pepper flakes**
1	**scallion, finely chopped**

NOODLES

1/2 pound	**spaghetti**
1/2 cup	**tamari** (dark soy sauce), **eyeball it**
3 rounded tablespoons	**smooth peanut butter**
2 tablespoons	**cider or rice vinegar**
2 tablespoons	**vegetable oil, eyeball it**
2 teaspoons	**dark sesame oil, eyeball it**
1/2 teaspoon	**cayenne pepper**
1 cup	**shredded cabbage and carrot mix** (available preshredded in produce department)
1 cup	**bean sprouts, any variety** (available in produce department)
2	**scallions, chopped on an angle**
2 tablespoons	**sesame seeds**

Bake spring rolls according to package directions. Meanwhile, make the dipping sauce: Stir together the plum or duck sauce, tamari, sesame oil, red-pepper flakes, and scallions in a small bowl.

MAKE YOUR OWN TAKE-OUT

Make the noodles: Cook pasta according to package direction, to al dente (with a "bite" to it, or slightly chewy) then run it under cold water in a colander to stop the cooking process. Drain the pasta very well.

In the bottom of a large bowl, whisk together tamari, peanut butter, vinegar, vegetable oil, sesame oil, and cayenne pepper. Add noodles, cabbage, bean sprouts, and scallions and toss to combine and coat the noodles evenly with sauce. Sprinkle sesame seeds throughout the salad and serve.

CHEESY Smashed Potatoes

■ **Makes 4 servings**

2 to 2 + 1/4 pounds	**baby Yukon gold potatoes**
	Salt and freshly ground black pepper, to taste
1/4 cup	**sour cream**
2 cups	**shredded cheddar cheese**
3 tablespoons	**chopped or snipped chives**

Cut potatoes in half and place in a pot. Cover potatoes with water and bring to a boil. Work on other dishes while you are waiting for the water to boil.

When water boils, add 2 big pinches salt; boil potatoes 10 minutes or until tender. Go work on other stuff again.

Drain potatoes and return them to the hot pot. Smash potatoes with a masher and combine with sour cream and cheese. When cheese melts into potatoes, add chives, salt, and pepper, and re-smash. Taste the potatoes and adjust seasonings.

meat & potatoes
menu for the
next great chef

cheesy
smashed potatoes

grilled t-bone steaks
with chipotle-chili rub
and cilantro-lime
compound butter

sauteed veggies
for steak

I designed this menu for my friend Harry who is just starting high school this year. He grew up in a gourmet market. I worked with his mom and dad. Harry is too cool. He plays the electric guitar, he's really cute, and he loves to cook! Look out girls! Harry might be the first rock star chef, so I thought I would write a menu that rocked, too. It's full of info and tricks-of-the-trade so he'll know a thing or two ahead of time if he goes to culinary school one day.

Grilled T-Bone Steaks with Chipotle-Chili Rub and Cilantro-Lime Compound Butter

■ **Makes 4 servings, plus extra reserved compound butter**

1	**lime**
1 cup	**butter, cut into chunks** (2 sticks)
3 tablespoons	**finely chopped cilantro**
4	**T-bone steaks, 1 + 1/2 inch thick**
2 tablespoons	**steak seasoning blend for the grill, such as Montreal Seasoning by McCormick**
1 tablespoon	**chipotle** (smoky) **ground chili powder or dark chili powder**
1 tablespoon	**sweet paprika**

Preheat a two-burner grill pan over high heat or a tabletop electric grill to high, or preheat the outdoor grill. Grate the zest of the lime (the green part of the skin—not the white part) on the small holes of a grater. Cut the lime in half crosswise and squeeze all the juice from the lime halves into a bowl.

Place butter in a microwave-safe bowl. Place bowl in microwave and cook on high for 15 seconds. Stir in cilantro and lime zest and juice using a rubber spatula. Transfer the butter onto a large piece of plastic wrap.

Gather the ends of the plastic wrap in one hand and use a straight edge, like a small cookie sheet pan, to push the butter back and away from your body making the butter take on a log shape.

Gently roll the log wrapped in plastic back and forth on the countertop to evenly round out the shape. Twist up the extra wrap on the ends and place the compound butter log into the freezer to make the butter cold enough to slice again.

Remove the steaks from the refrigerator and unwrap. Combine the steak seasoning blend with ground chipotle pepper (smoked jalapeño powder) and sweet paprika. A tablespoon is about a palmful of powdered or ground seasonings. Rub the seasoning blend into the steaks, distributing the spices evenly among them. Go wash your hands. Using tongs, place steaks on screaming-hot grill, carefully place the thin tip of one steak facing the wide end of the next so that all 4 steaks fit onto the grill at the same time. Cook steaks 6 to 7 minutes on each side for medium doneness. Remove steaks and let them rest so that the juices can redistribute, 5 minutes.

When ready to serve, top steaks with discs of sliced compound butter, and serve with salad or vegetables on the side. The cheesy smashed potatoes (page before) and sautéed veggies (following) make especially tasty side dishes for these steaks.

SAUTÉED VEGGIES for Steak

■ **Makes 4 BIG veggie servings**

2 tablespoons	**extra-virgin olive oil (evoo)** (2 turns of the pan)
1 pound	**large white mushrooms, sliced**
1	**red bell pepper**
1	**yellow bell pepper**
1/2 large	**red onion**
	Salt and freshly ground black pepper, to taste
2 tablespoons	**cilantro-lime compound butter** (recipe above)

Heat a large skillet over medium-high heat. Add evoo. Add sliced mushrooms and let them brown. While the mushrooms cook, cut the peppers in half and pull out the seeds and connective membranes and throw them away. Cut peppers into quarters lengthwise, then slice across. Cut onion in half lengthwise and peel it. Wrap half and save it for another use. Cut off ends and cut the half onion lengthwise in half again. Then, slice the onions across. Add peppers and onions to mushrooms and season with salt and pepper. Cook veggies another 3 to 5 minutes, stirring often, until they're just tender, but still have a little crunch left to them and lots of bright color. Remove veggies from the heat and add cilantro-lime butter. Toss veggies to melt butter, then serve.

Spaghetti and Meatball STOUP

■ **Makes 4 servings**

ONE-POT WONDER

2 tablespoons	**extra-virgin olive oil (evoo)** (2 turns of the pan)
1	**carrot, peeled and chopped into small dice**
1 small	**yellow onion, chopped**
3 cloves	**garlic, chopped**
2 cups	**tomato sauce**
4 cups	**chicken stock**
1 pound	**ground beef, pork, and veal mix** (meatloaf mix) (available at butcher counter)
1/2 cup	**grated Parmigiano Reggiano or Romano cheese** (a couple of handfuls), **plus more to pass at table**
1/2 cup	**Italian bread crumbs** (a few handfuls)
1 large	**egg, beaten**
2 tablespoons	**chopped fresh flat-leaf parsley**
1/2 pound	**spaghetti, broken in half**
1 cup	**basil leaves, torn or shredded**
1 loaf	**crusty Italian bread, for dunking**

Preheat a medium soup pot over medium heat. Add evoo, carrots, onions, and garlic, and sauté 5 minutes. Add tomato sauce and chicken stock and cover pot. Turn up heat and bring to a fast boil.

While soup comes to a boil, mix the ground meat with cheese, bread crumbs, egg, and parsley. Roll into 1 & 1/2- to 2-inch balls.

Remove lid from soup and slide balls into soup. Bring back to a boil then stir in spaghetti. Reduce the heat and simmer soup 10 minutes more, until pasta is tender and balls are cooked through. Stir in basil and remove from heat. Serve with bread and extra cheese.

Vegetable Chili STOUP with Baked Quesadillas!

■ **Makes 4 servings**

ONE-POT WONDER

2 tablespoons	**extra-virgin olive oil (evoo) or vegetable oil** (2 turns of the pan)
1 medium	**yellow onion, chopped**
1	**carrot, peeled and diced**
1 large	**red or green bell pepper, seeded and chopped**
1 large	**jalapeño pepper, seeded and chopped**
2 cloves	**garlic, chopped**
1 small	**zucchini, chopped**
1 tablespoon	**ground cumin** (a palmful)
2 tablespoons	**chili powder** (2 palmfuls)
1 tablespoon	**cayenne pepper sauce, such as Frank's Red Hot**
	Salt, to taste
1 can	**crushed tomatoes** (14 ounces)
4 cups	**vegetable or chicken stock**
1 can	**black beans, rinsed and drained** (14 ounces)
1 can	**dark red kidney beans, rinsed and drained** (14 ounces)
8	**flour tortillas** (8-inch)
2 + 1/2 cups	**shredded cheddar or Monterey Jack cheese** (one 10-ounce sack, preshredded is available on dairy aisle)
2	**scallions, chopped**

Preheat oven to 400°F.

Make the stoup: Preheat a soup pot over medium-high heat. Add oil, onions, carrot, bell pepper, jalapeño, garlic, and zucchini. Sauté 10 minutes, add cumin, chili powder, cayenne sauce, and salt; stir. Add tomatoes, stock, and beans and bring soup to a boil. Lower heat and simmer 10 minutes.

Make the quesadillas: Get out 2 cookie sheets and place 2 tortillas next to each other on each cookie sheet. Cover each tortilla with 1/2 cup cheese and a few pieces of chopped scallions, then place a tortilla on top of each. Bake 5 minutes to melt cheese and crisp tortillas. Cut quesadillas into 4 wedges each to make a total of 4 quesadilla rounds, 4 wedges per person.

Serve veggie chili stoup with quesadilla wedges for dipping.

Creamy Tomato-Basil MUG-o-SOUP

■ Makes 4 mugs and toppers

2 cups	**whole milk**
2 cans	**diced tomatoes, drained (14 ounces each)**
2 rounded tablespoons	**tomato paste**
1 medium	**yellow onion, chopped**
	Salt and freshly ground pepper, to taste
1 teaspoon	**sugar**
3 tablespoons	**all-purpose flour**
2 tablespoons	**butter, cut into pieces** (tablespoons are marked on the wrapper)
1/2 stalk	**celery, coarsely chopped**
2	**sandwich-size English muffins, split**
1 clove	**garlic, cracked with a heavy pan**
	Extra-virgin olive oil (evoo), for drizzling
1/2 cup	**grated Parmigiano Reggiano or Romano cheese**
	Dried Italian seasoning blend, any brand
1/2 cup	**fresh basil leaves, torn or shredded**

Heat milk to a simmer over medium heat in a medium pot. Put tomatoes, tomato paste, onions, salt, pepper, sugar, flour, butter, and celery into a food processor and grind until smooth. Pour mixture into milk and raise heat to bring soup to a boil. Reduce heat and simmer 15 minutes.

Toast English muffins. Rub with cracked garlic and drizzle with evoo. Top muffins with cheese and a pinch of dried Italian seasoning, then melt and brown cheese under broiler or in a toaster oven.

Stir fresh basil into soup and adjust seasonings. Pour soup into mugs and cap mugs with a garlic-muffin mug topper.

Clam Chowda MUG·O·SOUP with Deviled Ham and Cheese Melt Mug Toppers

■ **Makes 4 mugs and toppers**

2 tablespoons	**butter** (tablespoons are marked on the wrapper)
2 slices	**bacon, chopped**
1 medium	**yellow onion, chopped**
1 stalk	**celery, chopped**
4 sprigs	**fresh thyme**
	Salt and freshly ground pepper, to taste
2 tablespoons	**all-purpose flour**
1 cup	**frozen shredded hash brown potatoes** (available in sacks on dairy aisle)
1 cup	**cream**
2 cups	**chicken stock**
2 cans	**whole baby clams with their juice**
2	**sandwich-size English muffins, split**
1/2 pound	**boiled deli ham, chopped**
1 teaspoon	**paprika**
2 teaspoons	**hot sauce, such as Frank's Red Hot**
1 tablespoon	**yellow or brown mustard**
A handful of	**fresh flat-leaf parsley**
8 deli slices	**sharp cheddar cheese**

In a medium pot over medium-high heat melt butter. Add bacon, onions, celery, and thyme sprigs. Season with salt and pepper and cook 5 minutes. Add flour and cook a minute more.

Add potatoes and stir to combine. Add cream, chicken stock, and clams. Bring soup to a boil, then lower to a simmer, 15 minutes.

Toast English muffins. While muffins toast, grind ham with paprika, hot sauce, mustard, and parsley in a food processor. Spread ham on toasted muffins. Top each muffin half with 2 slices cheddar cheese and melt cheese in toaster oven or under broiler.

Remove the thyme stems from the soup (the leaves will have fallen off into the soup). Stir and adjust seasonings. Serve with deviled-ham–and-cheese mug toppers.

Chicken Mug Pie

■ **Makes 4 mugs**

1 tube	**jumbo butter biscuits, such as Grands by Pillsbury** (available in dairy aisle)
	Sweet paprika, for sprinkling
2 tablespoons	**butter** (tablespoons are marked on the wrapper)
2	**single chicken breasts** (6–8 ounces each), **chopped**
1 stalk	**celery, chopped**
1 medium	**yellow onion, chopped**
1 large	**carrot, diced**
	Salt and freshly ground pepper, to taste
2 teaspoons	**poultry seasoning**
2 tablespoons	**all-purpose flour**
1 cup	**frozen shredded hash browns potatoes** (available in sacks on dairy aisle)
1 cup	**cream**
1 quart	**chicken stock**
1 cup	**frozen green peas**

Preheat oven according to package directions and arrange biscuits on cookie sheet. Sprinkle with a little paprika and bake, 10 to 12 minutes.

In a medium pot over medium to medium-high heat, melt butter, then cook chicken in butter, 2 minutes; add celery, onions, and carrots, and season with salt, pepper, and poultry seasoning. Cook 5 minutes more; add flour and cook another minute. Add potatoes, cream, and chicken stock. Bring soup to a boil by raising heat, then turn heat back to simmer and cook soup another 10 minutes. Stir in peas and cook 1 minute to warm them through.

Serve mugs of soup with biscuits on top to cap the mug: chicken mug pies!

SPiCY Honey-Nut Chicken

■ **Makes 4 servings**

4 ounces	**honey-roasted peanuts** (2 small packages or about 2/3 cup)
1/2 cup	**store-bought plain bread crumbs**
1 tablespoon	**grill seasoning blend, such as Montreal Seasoning by McCormick**
1	**egg**
A splash of	**half-and-half or whole milk**
2 teaspoons	**hot sauce** (several drops), **such as Frank's Red Hot**
1/2 cup	**all-purpose flour**
2–3 tablespoons	**vegetable oil** (2 to 3 turns of the pan)
4	**boneless, skinless chicken breast halves** (6–8 ounces each)

Preheat oven to 350°F.

Put peanuts, bread crumbs, and grill seasoning in a food processor and pulse-grind to combine. Pour nutty breading onto a plate.

Beat egg and half-and-half or milk with hot sauce in a shallow dish.

Pour flour out onto a plastic board or plate.

Preheat a nonstick skillet over medium-high heat. Add oil to coat the bottom of the pan with a thin layer. Brown chicken in hot oil until evenly light golden in color, about 2 minutes on each side. Transfer chicken to a baking sheet and cook in oven until juices run clear and breasts are cooked through, 10 to 12 minutes.

Barbecued Succotash

1 tablespoon	**extra-virgin olive oil (evoo) or vegetable oil** (1 turn of the pan)
1/2	**red onion, chopped**
1	**red bell pepper, seeded and chopped**
1 can	**black beans, rinsed and drained** (14 ounces)
1 box	**frozen corn** (10 ounces)
	Salt and freshly ground pepper, to taste
1/4 cup	**smoky barbecue sauce, any brand**
2 tablespoons	**chopped fresh chives, flat-leaf parsley, or cilantro, for garnish**

Heat a medium skillet over medium-high heat. Warm the oil, then add onions and peppers; sauté 5 minutes. Add beans and corn and season with salt and pepper. When corn heats through, add barbecue sauce. Stir to combine and serve succotash with chopped chives, parsley, or cilantro to garnish.

Honey, Spice, and Everything Nice Menu

Spicy Honey-Nut Chicken

Barbecued Succotash

Meatball Patty Melts

■ **Makes 4 patty melts**

1 pound	**ground sirloin**
1	**egg, beaten**
1/4 small	**yellow onion, finely chopped or grated with a hand grater**
2 cloves	**garlic, chopped**
1/2 cup	**grated parmesan or Romano cheese**
1/2 cup	**store-bought Italian bread crumbs**
	Salt and freshly ground pepper, to taste
2 tablespoons	**chopped fresh flat-leaf parsley**
1 tablespoon	**extra-virgin olive oil (evoo)**
1 tablespoon	**butter** (tablespoons are marked on the wrapper)
8 slices	**Italian bread, such as semolina bread**
8 deli slices	**provolone cheese**
2 cups	**pizza sauce or marinara sauce**

Mix meat, egg, onion, garlic, cheese, bread crumbs, salt, pepper, and parsley. Form 4 large patties.

Heat a large nonstick skillet over medium-high heat and pour in evoo. Cook patties 5 minutes on each side. Remove from pan and wipe pan out with a paper towel.

Return skillet to heat and melt butter over medium-low heat. Add 4 slices bread and place a slice of cheese on each slice of bread. Top with patties, another slice of cheese, then put on top slices of bread. Cook melts 2 minutes on each side to toast bread and melt cheese.

Heat red sauce in small pot or in microwave. Cut sandwiches corner to corner. Serve each melt with 1/2 cup sauce in a small bowl on the side for dipping the sandwiches.

Here are 3 funky new recipes for everybody's American favorite: the burger! Serve any of them with a green salad or oil-and-vinegar-dressed cole slaw and some fancy chips from the gourmet or natural foods snack aisle.

Chicken Cordon Bleu BURGERS!

■ **Makes 4 half-pound burgers**

2 teaspoons	**vegetable or olive oil** (a drizzle)
4 slices	**Canadian bacon**
2 pounds	**ground chicken breast**
2 teaspoons	**sweet paprika, eyeball it in your palm**
2 teaspoons	**poultry seasoning**
2 teaspoons	**grill seasoning blend, such as Montreal Steak Seasoning, or salt and pepper**
1	**shallot, finely chopped**
	Extra-virgin olive oil (evoo), for drizzling
4 deli slices	**Swiss cheese**
2/3 cup	**mayonnaise, eyeball it**
3 rounded tablespoons	**Dijon mustard**
4 sprigs	**fresh tarragon, leaves stripped and chopped** (2 tablespoons)
4	**Kaiser rolls or sandwich-size sourdough English muffins, split and toasted**
8 leaves	**lettuce**
1	**vine-ripened tomato, thinly sliced**

Preheat a grill pan, nonstick griddle, large nonstick skillet, or table-top electric grill to medium-high heat. Add a drizzle of oil and the Canadian bacon. Cook bacon until caramelized (brown and bubbly) at edges, 1 to 2 minutes on each side. Remove to a piece of aluminum foil. Fold foil over loosely to keep warm.

Combine ground chicken, paprika, poultry seasoning, grill seasoning, and shallot. Score meat with the side of your hand to separate
into 4 equal amounts; make 4 large patties, 3/4 to 1 inch thick.
Drizzle patties with evoo and place on hot grill pan or griddle or in
skillet. Cook about 5 minutes on each side, until cooked through.

Top patties with reserved cooked Canadian bacon and Swiss
cheese, folding each slice of cheese in half to fit the burger. Cover
loosely with foil. Turn off pan and let cheese melt, 2 minutes.

Make the sauce: Combine mayo, mustard, and tarragon. Slather
bun tops with sauce. Place burgers on bun bottoms and top with
lettuce and tomato. Put bun tops in place.

Turkey Chili, Cheddar & Bacon BURGERS!

■ **Makes 4 servings**

8 slices	**applewood bacon or turkey bacon**
1 + 1/3 pounds	**ground turkey or ground turkey breast**
1/2 small	**red bell pepper, chopped**
3	**scallions, chopped**
2 teaspoons	**poultry seasoning**
2 tablespoons	**chipotle chile powder or 2 tablespoons dark chili powder mixed with 2 teaspoons ground cumin**
1 teaspoon	**salt, or to taste**
1 tablespoon	**vegetable oil (1 turn of the pan)**
4 thick deli slices	**cheddar cheese**
4	**crusty onion Kaiser rolls, split**
4 leaves	**lettuce**
1/2 cup	**barbecue sauce, any brand**

Broil the bacon or cook it in the microwave until crisp. To cook in the microwave, place 4 slices bacon per row between paper towels and cook 4 minutes on high; turkey bacon will only cook 2 to 3 minutes. To cook under broiler, place bacon on slotted pan and broil 6 inches from heat, 3 minutes on each side; turkey bacon will only cook 2 minutes per side. Drain cooked bacon and reserve.

Mix ground turkey with bell peppers, scallions, poultry seasoning, chipotle chile powder, and salt, and form 4 big patties. Heat a non-stick skillet over medium-high heat and cook patties in vegetable oil until cooked through, 5 or 6 minutes on each side. Melt cheese over burgers the last minute they are in the pan by tenting the pan loosely with foil.

Place bun bottoms on plates and top each with lettuce, cheeseburger, and 2 slices bacon. Spread a few tablespoons barbecue sauce on each bun top and set in place.

Index

Use this to search the book for ingredients or recipes by name!